ENGINEERING

MADE SIMPLE

Portable Press
An imprint of Printers Row Publishing Group
10350 Barnes Canyon Road, Suite 100, San Diego, CA 92121
www.portablepress.com • mail@portablepress.com

Copyright © 2020 Quarto Publishing plc

Printers Row Publishing Group is a division of Readerlink Distribution Services, LLC.
Portable Press is a registered trademark of Readerlink Distribution Services, LLC.

Correspondence regarding the content of this book should be sent to Portable Press, Editorial Department, at the above address. Author, illustration, and rights inquiries should be sent to Quarto Publishing plc, 6 Blundell Street, London, N7 9BH, www.quartoknows.com.

Portable Press
Publisher: Peter Norton • Associate Publisher: Ana Parker
Senior Developmental Editor: April Graham Farr
Editor: Dan Mansfield
Product Manager: Kathryn Chipinka Dalby

Produced by Quarto Publishing plc
Publisher: James Evans
Editorial Director: Isheeta Mustafi
Managing Editor: Jacqui Sayers
Editors: Katie Crous and Abbie Sharman
Art Director: Katherine Radcliffe
Designers: Tall Tree and Subtract Design
Additional content: Helen Heggie

Library of Congress Control Number: 2020934557
ISBN: 978-1-64517-255-0

Printed in China

24 23 22 21 20   1 2 3 4 5

Cover credits:
Cover Design: Greg Stalley
Cover Images: Shutterstock

ENGINEERING

MADE SIMPLE

A COMPLETE GUIDE IN TEN EASY LESSONS

MICHAEL McRAE &
JONATHAN BERLINER

PORTABLE
PRESS

San Diego, California

CONTENTS

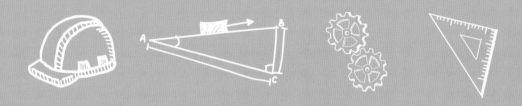

INTRODUCTION

This book is brought to you by a long list of engineers. Mechanical engineers designed the devices that printed ink on the pages. Chemical engineers formulated the ink and made the paper smooth and shiny. Computer engineers wrote the programs that set out the design and allowed the authors to type the words. Without them, books like this—all books, in fact—wouldn't be possible.

In fact, just about everything that is manufactured today is a product of engineering; from the way we travel to the clothes we wear, to what we do to have fun. Medicine, food, sports equipment, cosmetics, rockets, and buildings—they have all been designed, tested, built, maintained, and will be broken down and recycled by engineers.

Engineering is the application of science and mathematics in design and construction. Buildings and machines might be the first things that come to mind, but it can just as easily be applied to rearranging molecules or even living tissues.

Today, engineers can cover a variety of disciplines. To get a rocket into orbit, for example, there are chemical engineers devising strong, lightweight materials that can withstand the pressures of space travel. There are mechanical engineers figuring out how to arrange the materials to handle extreme forces. There are electrical engineers connecting sensors and communications technology, computer engineers coming up with programs to read the data they send back . . .

Wherever equations and theories have been used to create a practical solution, we can say engineering has played a pivotal role. Engineers have to know a lot of mathematics and science, but perhaps most importantly, they all need to work together to be successful.

History is full of examples of clever answers to life's little—and often enormous—challenges. This book tells the story of just a few of them. And behind every one of those solutions, there is a discovery or two that showed us how the universe works. This book will also explain the science that underpins a vast variety of engineering fields.

It's not just history we need to think about, though. Our future is full of problems that will need to be solved. And those future problems will need clever thinkers to come up with engineering solutions. Who knows, maybe one of them is holding this book in their hands right now.

ABOUT THIS BOOK

This comprehensive guide covers the key concepts of engineering. From a general look at the subject—what it involves and influences, and how it works—to examining its numerous applications in the world around us, this book will guide you methodically through this vast field. The featured lessons offer insight into the workings of buildings, power, transportation, machines, chemical processes, bioengineering, and communications. The book ends with a journey into the future of engineering's predicted areas of development and a technology timeline. Throughout the book there are various features that will help guide you and deepen your understanding:

- ## LESSON INTRODUCTION

At the start of each lesson is a handy introduction that outlines the key learning points.

FACT Most topics have an intriguing fact highlighted in an easy-to-see box.

QUIZ TIME

Find these quizzes at the end of each lesson and grade yourself on your understanding and progress before moving on to the next lesson.

SIMPLE SUMMARY

At the end of each lesson is a summary that recaps the topics covered.

ANSWER THIS

At the end of each topic is a spot test, which should help to assess whether you have fully understood the topic and how to apply it in real-life situations. Try to answer these questions immediately after reading the relevant pages, without peeking at the text for answers.

- ## ANSWERS

Turn to the back of the book for answers to all the tests—no peeking now!

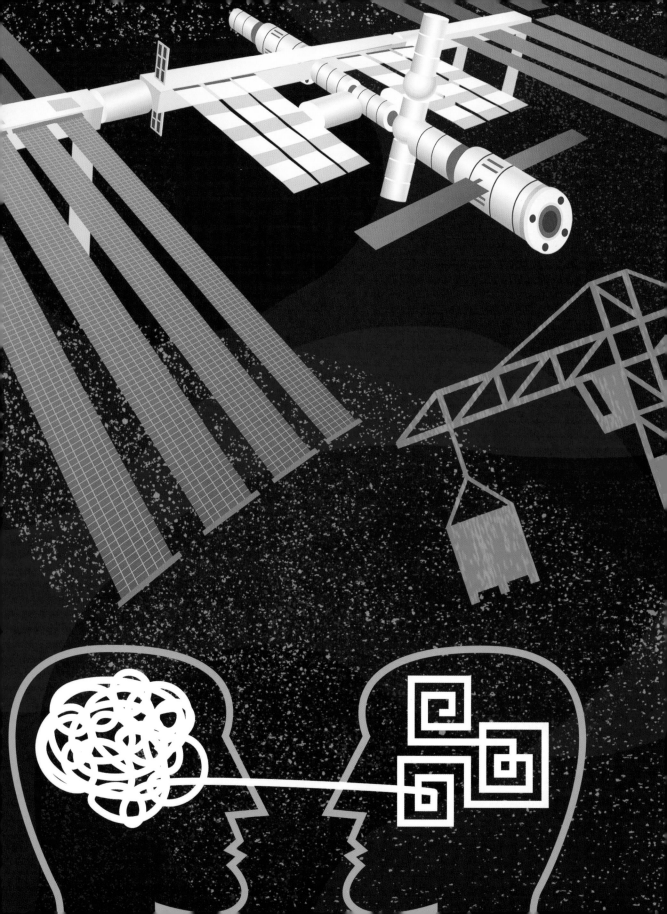

1

WHAT IS ENGINEERING?

Engineers create things because something is needed.
A problem needs solving: a river needs crossing, more food
needs to be grown, or someone needs to be rescued from a
seemingly unreachable place. This is how the first engineers
started, by finding solutions to problems. Modern
engineering has built on these foundations to lead us
into a technological era.

WHAT YOU WILL LEARN

Discovery and invention

Skill set

Economics of engineering

Risks and safety

Who are engineers?

Making measurements

DISCOVERY AND INVENTION

We know from archaeological excavations in Mesopotamia that the first known wheel is said to have been invented back in 3500 BC. This earliest form of engineering development was created to make it easier to move—ourselves or heavy loads—around. Over the years, this idea was taken and adapted, improved, extended, and added to by engineers until today, over 5,000 years later, we have supercars that can travel at over 300 miles per hour!

Engineering is the application of science. As scientific understanding has, and continues to, expand, we are finding out more and more about the world in which we live. For instance, most inventions are not new at all, but are the development of an existing idea or concept to make something

FACT

Some inventions over time have had a huge impact on the way humans live. These game-changers include the first electric light bulb, invented in 1809 by Humphry Davy, or the identification of the first antibiotic, penicillin, by Alexander Fleming in 1928.

TIMELINE OF THE WHEEL

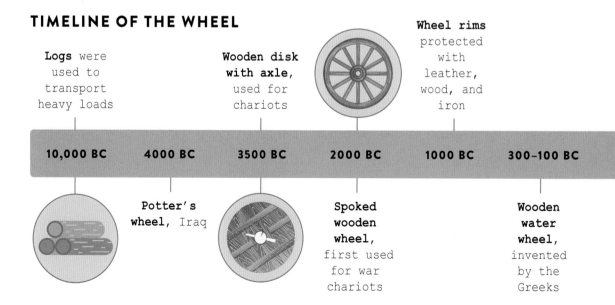

Logs were used to transport heavy loads

Wooden disk with axle, used for chariots

Wheel rims protected with leather, wood, and iron

| 10,000 BC | 4000 BC | 3500 BC | 2000 BC | 1000 BC | 300–100 BC |

Potter's wheel, Iraq

Spoked wooden wheel, first used for war chariots

Wooden water wheel, invented by the Greeks

uniquely better. The handy electronic calculator started its life as an abacus in ancient times—beads on a row of sticks to count and add up complex numbers. The mobile phone began from relaying messages via pigeon or messenger. Music streaming to personal devices developed from records played via gramophones, to records, tape cassettes, compact discs, then downloads. Everything that is made in our world has followed an engineering evolution, starting out simple and then made better and better by generations of engineers and scientists.

Patents

In modern times, if engineers or scientists have a really good idea and invent or improve something in a revolutionary way, they protect their idea to prevent someone else from copying their exact design. By registering an idea, the designer or inventor protects the invention for a number of years, and therefore gains the benefit, by being the only person able to make and sell whatever they have registered. This recording of a design is called "filing a patent." The first patent was recorded in Florence, Italy, in 1421 by engineer Filippo Brunelleschi, who received a three-year patent for a special barge that was built to carry heavy marble. Patent law first came about in the United States in 1790, and even though some inventions were discovered by several people at the same time, the first person to get a patent recorded and registered would be the only person able to use and sell the invention or discovery for a long period of time. This, at times, could cause lawsuits and many arguments!

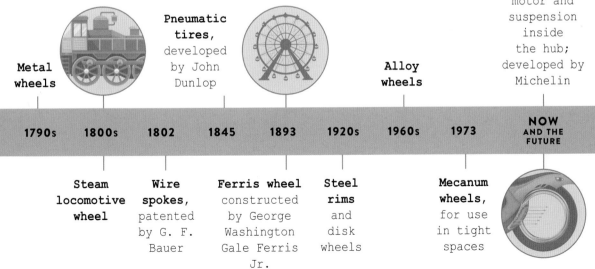

Hubless wheel: Hollow wheel with no axle or center hub; for motorcycles
Tweel: Airless tire from Michelin
Active wheel: Houses an electric motor and suspension inside the hub; developed by Michelin

Metal wheels

Pneumatic tires, developed by John Dunlop

Alloy wheels

| 1790s | 1800s | 1802 | 1845 | 1893 | 1920s | 1960s | 1973 | **NOW AND THE FUTURE** |

Steam locomotive wheel

Wire spokes, patented by G. F. Bauer

Ferris wheel constructed by George Washington Gale Ferris Jr.

Steel rims and disk wheels

Mecanum wheels, for use in tight spaces

1.2 SKILL SET

Engineers need to have good knowledge of science, technology, engineering, and math, or "STEM." Engineers need to understand the science around how things work, interact, and react in order to determine what is going on and to create a solution.

What do you think of when you hear the word "skills"? Maybe you play a team sport and recognize skills as something you get if you practice and become good. Maybe you play chess or strategy games and have skills that come from being logical or analyzing lots of information and making decisions. Well, engineers also need skills. They develop their skills by practicing and working on different projects with different people.

So, what skills do engineers need? An engineer's role is to come up with solutions to problems, invent new creative products, and to help keep us safe, warm, fed, and healthy. To solve problems, therefore, engineers will ask lots of questions, communicate ideas, work in teams, and, importantly, be able to apply their science and technical knowledge to come up with a solution.

Think about it. What good would it be having an idea if you could not tell other people about it? What would happen if you had to solve a critical problem in a certain time, but you missed the deadline and

ANSWER THIS

1. What is the name for the skills that engineers need?

2. Name three skills that you already have.

3. What does STEM stand for?

4. Fill in the blanks: A good____ needs a ____ of different skills.

5. List all the employability skills. Can you think of any more?

it had serious consequences? The ability to work on a team, problem solve, plan, and organize are essential skills. We call these "employability skills."

The Team

Let's think about playing on a team. How does a good team work? What would happen if all of the players on a soccer or netball team were goalkeepers, or if all of them were defenders? It wouldn't work. A team works well if there is a mix of skills, where different people have different roles and all contribute to the performance of the team.

It is the same with engineers. Most engineers work on a team with other people who bring a mix of different skills to that team. There will be someone with excellent timekeeping skills, someone who keeps their eye on the money and is good with numbers, someone who comes up with wacky solutions, and others who can take those ideas and communicate them in a way that is easy to understand, that can put them into practice and make ideas real.

Think about what you are good at. If you asked your friends, what would they say about you? Are you a team player? Are you good at timekeeping? Are you the creative one who comes up with those wacky ideas that just might work? Or are you the leader who organizes everyone? Which skills that make a good engineer do you already have, and which could you develop?

MADE SIMPLE
TEAMWORK

A soccer team would not work well if they had 10 attackers (yellow team). Teamwork works better when you have players in the positions they are best skilled at, all doing different jobs (purple team).

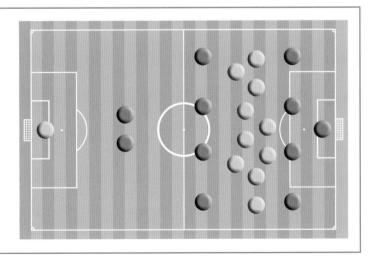

EMPLOYABILITY SKILLS

**1. Using initiative and being
self-motivated**
"Go get 'em!"

2. Organization
Plan and keep to the plan

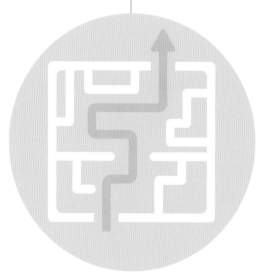

**5. Problem solving/
creative thinking**
Brilliant ideas = cool solutions

3. Working to deadlines
Say how long something will take and then do the task in that time

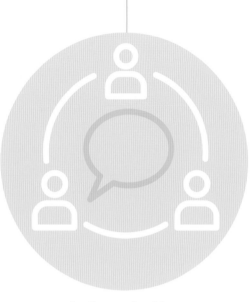

4. Communication
Be able to show people what you mean; draw/speak/write/illustrate your ideas

6. Numeracy/IT
Be able to understand costs, apply math, and be accurate with calculations

7. Teamwork
Work with others and each contribute to a good outcome

LESSON 1.3

ECONOMICS OF ENGINEERING

Engineering and inventing start with an initial idea, but that is just the beginning. After that first spark of brilliance, engineers must figure out how to turn that idea into reality. Numbers are important in engineering in lots of ways—math is key, and knowing how to work with numbers is essential within engineering. It needs to add up!

So you have had your brilliant idea. What things do you have to consider? If the idea is a building or a bridge, or some other large construction, engineers have to undertake calculations to ensure the design is safe, determine how much the raw materials will cost, estimate how much it will cost to build (the budget), how long it will take (time is money!), and then keep track of the costs to make sure the project stays within budget. If the idea is a product, engineers need to turn their idea into an item that will sell. There must be customers for the new product and a big enough demand, so that large enough quantities are sold, making the manufacturer a profit.

FACT

One of the most expensive single items ever built by a team of engineers, and the largest ever in space, is the International Space Station. It has cost more than $150 billion, and has been designed and made by engineers from several countries. The space station can be seen shining in the night sky. That is one superstar engineering project!

Cost-saving calculations

Some engineers' work is focused on making things cheaper. Engineers may look at a product and figure out how to reduce the manufacturing costs, reduce maintenance costs to make it more economical, or cut costs by being creative and modifying the design. This is called cost saving, and it allows products to be made more affordable and/or more profitable.

As well as undertaking calculations to ensure a design works or is "fit for purpose," engineers need to understand the economics, or finances, of their work. If the engineering team gets its calculations wrong, it could be expensive—building a bridge that is late being completed can cost millions, as there are often fines that need to be paid if a project is not finished on time.

It must, therefore, be worthwhile to make, produce, store, ship, sell, and use any new idea or product around the world, or else the project will not be able to happen.

MEGAPROJECTS

These extensive ventures typically cost over $1 billion or more, take many years to develop and build, involve multiple partners, transform lives, and impact millions of people.

JFK AIRPORT, NEW YORK
$10.3

CHANNEL TUNNEL, DOVER TO CALAIS
$15.4

AIRBUS A380 DEVELOPMENT PROJECT
$22

DUBAILAND THEME PARK
$64

INTERNATIONAL SPACE STATION, TO DATE
$150+

| 20 | 40 | 60 | 80 | 100 | 120 | 140 | 160 |

COST IN BILLIONS

ANSWER THIS

1. What is the term used when engineers make products cheaper to manufacture?

2. What is the largest manufactured item in space called?

3. What is the difference in cost between the Dubailand Theme Park project and the Airbus A380 Development project?

4. Name two things that engineers need to consider when designing a bridge.

LESSON 1.4

RISKS AND SAFETY

Some items that are designed and produced by engineers are safety-critical. A safety-critical item is a product that, if it should fail or malfunction, could cause serious injury—or even death. Designs that are safety-critical must be engineered carefully, and measures put in place to avoid a disaster if something should fail. Such products could be part of an aircraft or medical equipment.

Are you any good at spotting mistakes or the odd one out? Do you pay attention to detail? Engineering is about details, and some details can be critical. Engineers work very hard to keep us safe.

They do this in three ways:
- Ensuring that new designs work and do not have any dangerous parts or use poor-quality materials. In making a design fit for purpose, engineers make certain the item will last for as long as is needed without breaking or failing.
- Testing products to confirm that they are safe and are designed to specification; meaning they are exactly as the engineers and designers have calculated.
- Making sure that environments are safe for people to be in—either a workplace or manufacturing facility where the products are being made, or buildings used by the general public, such as offices, swimming pools, schools, and libraries.

Engineers undertake design procedures to help them determine all the risks and be able to put ideas and plans in place to prevent anything untoward from happening. An FMEA (failure mode and effects analysis) is a process where engineers think about what would happen if anything goes wrong. Think about a domino run: if you knock over one domino, it causes the next one to fall and keeps going until the final one. Engineers must look at their designs as if they are making a domino run—what would be the result if one thing goes wrong, and then created a knock-on effect of problems and issues? Every single possibility must be looked into, considering the outcome each time a different domino collapse (or failure) occurrs.

QUALITY CONTROL LOOP

MAKE PRODUCT TO DESIGN SPECIFICATION

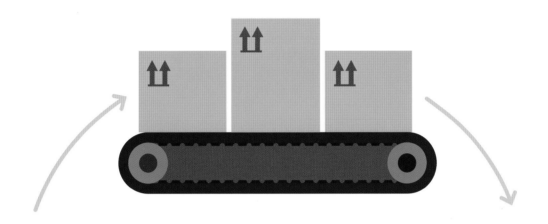

ADJUST THE PRODUCT

TEST

LOOK AT THE DATA

Quality control

Once a product is designed, there is a huge amount of engineering that still needs to be undertaken; from designing the machines to make the product, to monitoring production to ensure that each product is correctly made.

If some products are not accurately made, it is "not to the design specification," and they could go wrong once in use. This is a big issue. Aside from a lot of unhappy customers, if the fault is widespread and possibly dangerous, then the company would have to contact everyone that bought that item and ask them to return it. We call this a "recall," and it costs companies a huge amount of money.

Engineers must put quality control systems in place to check products carefully, removing any with issues, so they do not end up being sold to a customer. Manufacturing companies constantly test products as they are being made, analyzing the test data, then adjusting their machines if required. By carefully monitoring the products, companies make sure the quality is as expected, and that items will work properly.

FACT

The first factory inspectors were appointed under the Factory Act of 1833. Their main duty was to prevent injury and the overworking of children in the cotton/textile industry.

WHO ARE ENGINEERS?

Engineers look just like any of us. They are individuals who apply their STEM knowledge and employability skills in lots of different areas. Engineering may be based in science and technology, but it is an amazingly creative subject.

What are you interested in? Sports? Fashion? Music? Food? Engineers work in all these areas and more. Yet the question "What does an engineer do?" is quite tricky to answer. That is because engineering is everywhere, and engineers' jobs are incredibly varied.

BRANCHES OF ENGINEERING

Within engineering there are lots of different areas. Can you guess what engineers in these professional fields might do? Robotics, software, electrical, aerospace, nuclear, computer hardware, energy, agricultural, automotive, environmental . . . The list goes on.

CHEMICAL ENGINEERS
look at how to use basic raw materials to make products, such as plastics, cosmetics, paints, fuels. They study the chemistry but also how to undertake chemistry experiments on a huge scale, designing chemical plants and equipment.

One of the most common degrees studied by the heads of companies is engineering. This is because engineering helps develop problem-solving skills and understanding of how the world works.

Engineers could be spending their day testing race cars in wind tunnels, designing cosmetics for specific allergies, building space probes to investigate alien life, producing millions of cans of baked beans, or creating specialist medical equipment to monitor premature babies. Engineers work in all these fields.

What is common, though, is that whatever their job, in whatever environment, engineers are applying their STEM knowledge, coming up with creative solutions and figuring out how to turn these ideas into reality.

CIVIL ENGINEERS
design, build, operate, construct, and maintain roads, buildings, airports, tunnels, dams, bridges, and our water supply and sewage treatment systems.

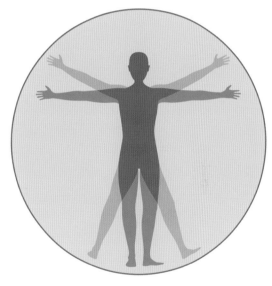

BIOMEDICAL ENGINEERS
focus on biomedical equipment and devices. This includes designing artificial internal organs, replacements for body parts, and machines for diagnosing medical problems. They work closely with medical professionals, doctors, and surgeons.

The future engineers

The world of STEM is growing at an exponential rate. As technology moves forward rapidly, our society needs more technologically advanced yet ethical products, services, and infrastructure. It is widely believed that we are now in the Fourth Industrial Revolution, where products are being linked together on a connected network, sharing data and communicating with one another, so who knows what the future will look like?

Engineers of the future will need to keep up that natural curiosity—keep asking "Why?" and exploring how our world works. They will need to challenge how we do things, to problem solve, and to think outside the box.

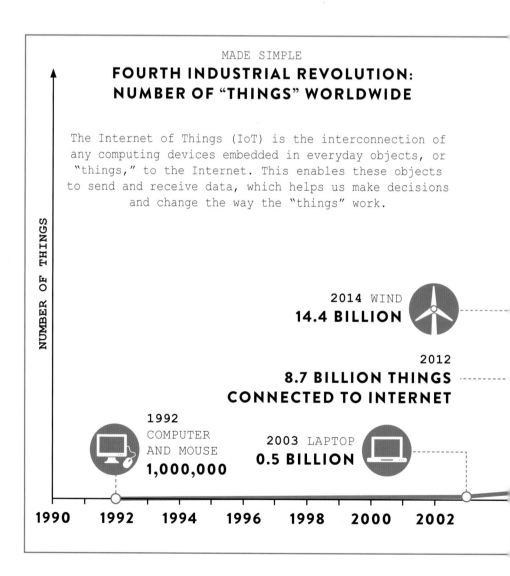

MADE SIMPLE
FOURTH INDUSTRIAL REVOLUTION: NUMBER OF "THINGS" WORLDWIDE

The Internet of Things (IoT) is the interconnection of any computing devices embedded in everyday objects, or "things," to the Internet. This enables these objects to send and receive data, which helps us make decisions and change the way the "things" work.

NUMBER OF THINGS

2014 WIND
14.4 BILLION

2012
8.7 BILLION THINGS CONNECTED TO INTERNET

1992
COMPUTER AND MOUSE
1,000,000

2003 LAPTOP
0.5 BILLION

1990   1992   1994   1996   1998   2000   2002

1. True or false: The rate that technology is increasing is slow and steady.

2. True or false: Engineering is about science and technology and does not involve arts/ creative subjects.

3. Can you name 10 fields of engineering from memory?

4. What type of engineer would create a robotic hand for someone with a missing limb?

5. Name four types of engineering projects that you might find a civil engineer working on.

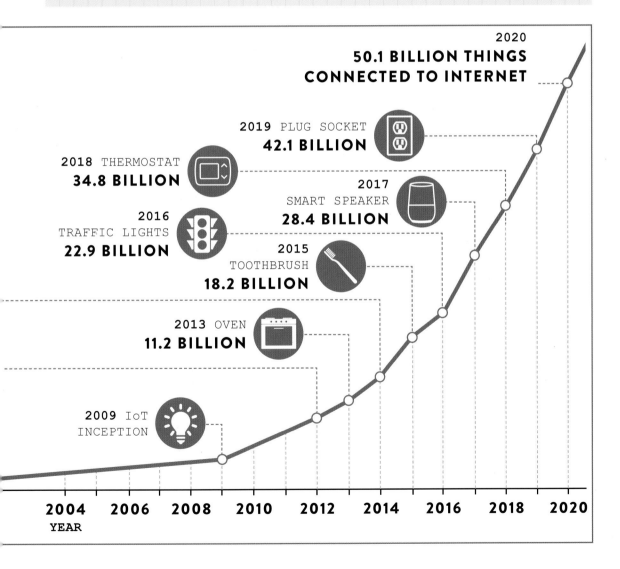

2020
50.1 BILLION THINGS CONNECTED TO INTERNET

2019 PLUG SOCKET
42.1 BILLION

2018 THERMOSTAT
34.8 BILLION

2017
SMART SPEAKER
28.4 BILLION

2016
TRAFFIC LIGHTS
22.9 BILLION

2015
TOOTHBRUSH
18.2 BILLION

2013 OVEN
11.2 BILLION

2009 IoT
INCEPTION

2004   2006   2008   2010   2012   2014   2016   2018   2020
YEAR

LESSON 1.6

MAKING MEASUREMENTS

Engineering over the centuries has improved as we've discovered how to measure our world in ever more precise ways. Different systems for measurement are used around the world, such as imperial and metric units. To avoid confusion, an International System of Units (SI) provides a standard of measurement for seven fundamental units that scientists and engineers use to communicate their ideas.

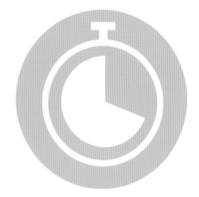

TIME
Base unit: Second (s)
Defined by the time it takes
for electrons in an atom of
cesium-133 in a special
state to shift
9,192,631,770 times.

LENGTH
Base unit: Meter (m)
Defined by the distance
light travels in a vacuum
in 1/299,792,458ths
of a second.

TEMPERATURE
Base unit: Kelvin (K)
In the 19th century, the Irish physicist William Thomson,
Lord Kelvin, calculated the lowest temperature possible was
-273 degrees Celsius. His scale is now defined by combining
the SI units for kilogram, meter, and second with a number
related to the energy of moving particles called the
Boltzmann constant.

MASS
Base unit: Kilogram (kg)
In the 19th century, a kilogram was anything that matched the weight of a metal cylinder kept in France. Now, it is defined by combining the SI units for time and length, with a number related to the energy carried by a single particle of light, called Planck's constant.

ELECTRIC CURRENT
Base unit: Ampere (A)
Defined by the flow of one coulomb per second. One coulomb is equal to about six quintillion electric charges.

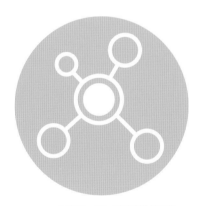

QUANTITY OF PARTICLES
Base unit: Mole (mol)
Defined by $6.02214076 \times 1,023$ particles.

BRIGHTNESS
Base unit: Candela (cd)
Defined by 1/683rd of a watt of light with a frequency $5.4 \times 1,014$ waves per second falling across a certain area.

WHAT IS ENGINEERING?

1. **What is the main reason that engineers create things?**

   a. Because they like science and technology

   b. Because they want to find out how things work

   c. Because there is a problem that needs solving

   d. Because engineers are practical

2. **Which of these must be the most important aspect of a design?**

   a. That it looks good

   b. That it is affordable

   c. That it is safe to use

   d. That it is better than anything that has been made before

3. **How much does a project have to cost to be classed as a megaproject?**

   a. More than $500,000

   b. More than $1 billion

   c. More than $10 billion

   d. More than $50 million

4. **How many things will be connected to the Internet by 2020, as our world becomes more connected and technology advances?**

   a. More than 50 billion things

   b. Over 20 million things

   c. None, as we will not have the technology to connect things

   d. Over 10 billion things

5. **From the first wheels invented, engineers and scientists have developed supercars that can now travel over 300 miles (480 km/h) per hour. How long has this taken?**

   a. 6,000 years

   b. 2,000 years

   c. 5,500 years

   d. 400 years

6. **What does FMEA stand for?**

   a. Find me every answer

   b. Failure mode and effects analysis

   c. Five mistakes eleven avoidances

   d. Fix my engineering attachment

7. **Which of these would an engineer NOT be involved in?**

   a. Developing a new form of transportation with zero emissions

   b. Creating a drilling machine to probe the seabed at extreme depths

   c. Designing safe ways to dispose of nuclear waste

   d. Producing a marketing campaign for a new soap

Answers on page 212

SIMPLE SUMMARY

Engineers create things because something is needed; a problem needs solving. Modern engineering has led us into a technological era.

- Most inventions are not new at all, but are the development of an existing idea or concept to make something uniquely better.

- The ability to work in a team, problem solve, plan, and organize are essential employability skills for engineers.

- Math is key, and knowing how to work with numbers is essential within engineering.

- Engineers work hard to keep us safe by ensuring that new designs are fit for purpose, testing products to confirm that they are safe and are designed to specification, and making sure that environments are safe for people to be in.

- Engineers apply their STEM knowledge, coming up with creative solutions and figuring out how to turn these ideas into reality.

- An International System of Units (SI) provides a standard of measurement for seven fundamental units that scientists and engineers use to communicate their ideas.

2
SCIENCE OF ENGINEERING

Whether designing airplanes, developing new pharmaceuticals, or genetically modifying bacteria, engineers can do their jobs more effectively if they know how the world around them works. Discovering the rules of nature is the job of scientists, who use experiments to test their ideas. Engineers can then use this knowledge to understand how their designs will work, and push technology to the limits of possibility.

WHAT YOU WILL LEARN

From science to technology

Engineering by numbers

Engineering for science

Pushing and pulling

Tiny building blocks

Balance of energy

FROM SCIENCE TO TECHNOLOGY

The idea of using experiments to test our understanding of nature first appeared in the writings of Ibn al-Haytham, who lived in Egypt at the turn of the 11th century, but it wasn't widely taken up until the 17th century. That time saw the invention of the telescope and the microscope, which helped test our understanding of nature to far greater depths.

Since then, science and engineering have become more sophisticated at an ever-increasing rate, allowing for structures to be taller, transportation to be faster, and enabling people to live twice as long on average as they did in the ancient world. Yet engineering has actually been around for thousands of years longer than science as we know it today.

Ancient knowledge

Ancient engineers had no scientific laws, but their practical knowledge allowed them to build structures such as Stonehenge in England, with stones weighing as much as 25 cars. To lift the stones into place, they would have

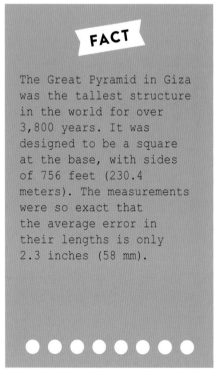

FACT

The Great Pyramid in Giza was the tallest structure in the world for over 3,800 years. It was designed to be a square at the base, with sides of 756 feet (230.4 meters). The measurements were so exact that the average error in their lengths is only 2.3 inches (58 mm).

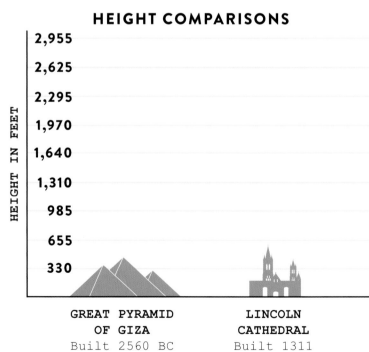

HEIGHT COMPARISONS

HEIGHT IN FEET

2,955
2,625
2,295
1,970
1,640
1,310
985
655
330

GREAT PYRAMID
OF GIZA
Built 2560 BC
481 FEET (146.5 M)

LINCOLN
CATHEDRAL
Built 1311
**524 FEET
(159.7 M)**

needed levers and pulleys, and would have had to predict the strength of the wood and rope with which they were made. Ancient engineers also knew that structures were more stable when wider at the bottom, which is why their tallest structures were pyramids, like those found in Egypt, Mexico, and Guatemala. These engineers also used a branch of mathematics called geometry, a word that comes from the Greek for "measuring the Earth," and their buildings often aligned with the positions of the Sun, Moon, and stars.

The engineers who designed the tallest building on Earth today, the Burj Khalifa in Dubai, had to be able to understand a lot more. Geologists studied the strength of the rocks beneath the tower, materials scientists studied how different concrete mixtures contract and expand at different temperatures, and physicists studied how gusts of wind would interact with the shape of the building. If they could not predict how the building would respond to a changing environment, it would be in danger of falling over.

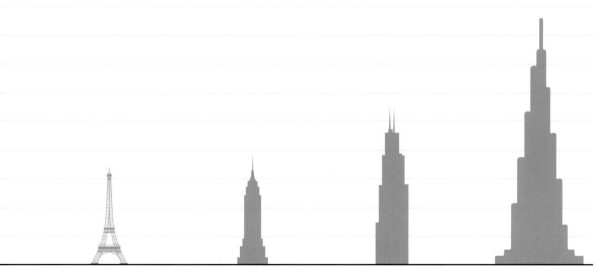

EIFFEL TOWER
Built 1889
1,063 FEET (324 M)

EMPIRE STATE BUILDING
Built 1931
1,250 FEET (381 M)

WILLIS TOWER
Built 1973
1,729 FEET (527 M)

BURJ KHALIFA
Built 2010
2,717 FEET (828 M)

LESSON 2.2 ENGINEERING BY NUMBERS

An engineer designing an artificial heart needs to know how fast blood will flow at different pressures, or the power needed to pump the right amount of blood. Anything can be given a number by taking measurements, such as the width of the tube or the electrical current. These numbers are used to find mathematical patterns and formulas that predict how engineered objects will work in the real world.

There is a legend that the ancient Greek mathematician Pythagoras was walking by a blacksmith's when he noticed that the hammer strikes were in tune with each other. When he inspected the hammers, he found their sizes were linked by a mathematical pattern. By describing the musical scale in numbers, he could make a rule that enables instrument makers to design instruments. Describing a situation in numbers and creating rules to describe how the numbers change is called modeling.

Geometry

Engineers use 3-D printers to make intricate parts for medical implants such as artificial hearts. The printer uses a mathematical model of where to print the plastic that builds up the shape. Geometry is the branch of mathematics that deals with modeling shapes by measuring angles, lengths, areas, and volumes. When medical engineers model blood flowing through an artery, they calculate its volume by multiplying the artery's three dimensions:

Volume = cross-sectional area × length

To calculate the artery's circular cross-sectional area, use the square of the circle's radius and the number 3.14159 (pi), normally written as π. Pi is the ratio of a circle's circumference to its diameter:

Volume = π × radius^2 × length

FACT

Engineers have been using π since ancient times but the first accurate method for calculating it was in 1400, and discovered by Mādhava, an Indian mathematician who calculated it to 11 decimal places. Modern computers use similar methods but can calculate to trillions of decimal places.

Units of measurement

Early civilizations understood the importance of agreeing on set units of measurements to compare the amounts of things. They used forearms, hands, and fingers for distances, and periods of the Sun or Moon for time. However, body parts change size from person to person, and they lacked accurate clocks to measure time. Now we can accurately measure distances as small as one 10-millionth of a millimeter, and times as short as one billionth of a second, making models and predictions more accurate too.

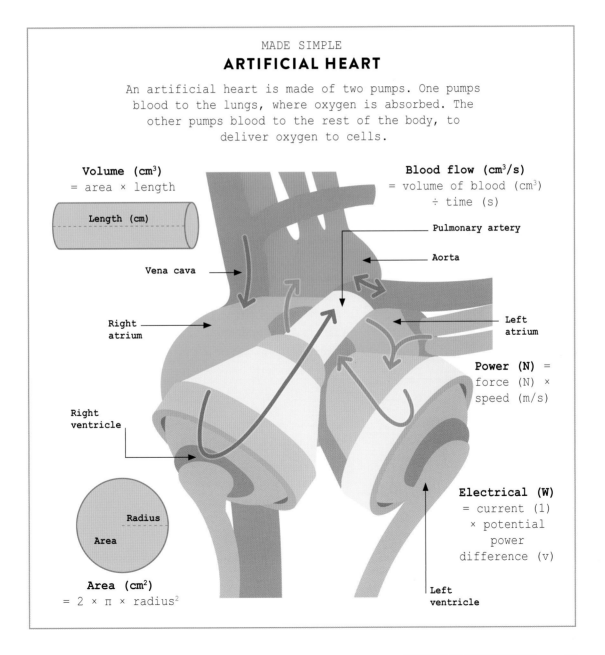

MADE SIMPLE
ARTIFICIAL HEART

An artificial heart is made of two pumps. One pumps blood to the lungs, where oxygen is absorbed. The other pumps blood to the rest of the body, to deliver oxygen to cells.

Volume (cm^3)
= area × length

Length (cm)

Blood flow (cm^3/s)
= volume of blood (cm^3)
÷ time (s)

Pulmonary artery

Aorta

Vena cava

Right atrium

Left atrium

Power (N) = force (N) × speed (m/s)

Right ventricle

Electrical (W)
= current (1) × potential power difference (v)

Radius

Area

Left ventricle

Area (cm^2)
= 2 × π × radius^2

LESSON 2.3

ENGINEERING FOR SCIENCE

Some of the biggest engineering projects are undertaken to build the experiments that probe the very smallest things we can measure, and they have pushed engineers to the limits of what is possible.

The Large Hadron Collider

The LHC is the world's best atom smasher. It accelerates a beam of protons with the width of a human hair to 99.999999 percent of the speed of light and is able to collide it with an equally fast, thin beam going the other way. To do this, a 17-mile (27-kilometer) ring of superconducting electromagnets is buried 328 feet (100 meters) under the ground. It can accurately track the debris from the trillions of collisions it can make in under a second, hoping to find new subatomic particles.

FACT

The Large Hadron Collider makes particles collide with so much energy that for a brief fraction of a second during the collision, it becomes the hottest place in the universe. A few inches away, however, the superconducting magnets that bend the path of the particles need to be so cold that they are one of the coldest places in the universe.

Neutrino detectors

There are billions of neutrinos going through your body every second, but we cannot feel them because neutrinos only very rarely interact with normal matter. Detectors have to be large to have the best chance of detecting something and need to be buried deep underground to avoid being set off by other radiation from space. Thousands of very sensitive light detectors surround the water and look for tiny flashes of light if a neutrino happens to interact.

The Extremely Large Telescope

The most advanced telescope in the world is well named. It has a 131-foot (40-meter) curved mirror to collect light from the sky and, although it has not been fully built yet, it will be able to capture 100 million times more light than the human eye. It will be used to discover distant planets by detecting tiny dips in light from stars as the planet goes in front of them.

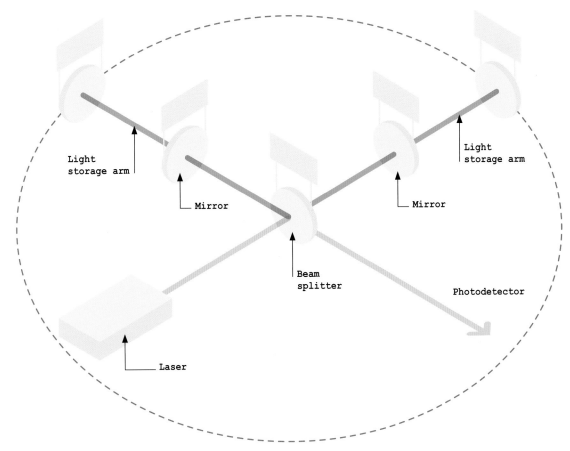

Light
storage arm

Mirror

Light
storage arm

Mirror

Beam
splitter

Photodetector

Laser

LIGO

The Laser Interferometer Gravitational-Wave
Observatory is in two locations in the United
States: Washington and Louisiana.

LIGO

Designed to detect tiny shifts in space-time
caused by gravitational waves, LIGO
reflects lasers down 2.5-mile- (4-kilometer-)
long vacuum chambers. It can sense shifts
that are smaller in length than a proton,
so any slight wobble from passing trains
or even distant earthquakes would affect
its measurements. Engineers have had
to come up with ways to keep the lasers
perfectly still.

ANSWER THIS

1. What is one reason
   for building the Large
   Hadron Collider?

2. Why do neutrino
   detectors have to
   be very large?

3. What is the main
   purpose of the
   Extremely Large
   Telescope?

4. What was LIGO built
   to detect?

PUSHING AND PULLING

In order to predict whether a bridge design will be stable, or how a new material will behave, engineers need to model how the objects, or the particles that they are made from, get pushed and pulled. Physicists call pushes and pulls "forces," and use formulas to model and predict how they affect objects as big as galaxies or as tiny as atoms.

In the late 17th century, English physicist Isaac Newton noticed that objects speed up in the direction in which they are being pushed or pulled.

The acceleration depends on how big the push and how heavy the object. A small push can make a bicycle go faster, but a car's engine pushes much more than a cyclist's legs.

NONCONTACT FORCES

The forces from gravity, electrostatic charge, and magnets can be felt at a distance. These are noncontact forces, and as the objects get farther apart, the forces get weaker.

MAGNETIC

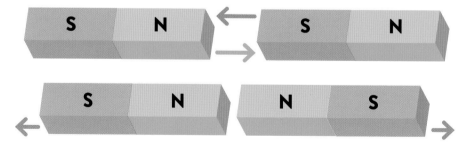

ELECTROSTATIC

Forces that are twice as big accelerate objects twice as much, or objects that are twice as heavy, so a force is calculated by multiplying the mass and acceleration:

Force (N) = mass (kg) × acceleration (m/s²)

When the mass or the acceleration get bigger, the formula makes the force bigger by the same amount. It agrees so closely with experiments that it is still used for everything from construction to space travel. The unit of measurement for a force is the newton (N).

GRAVITY

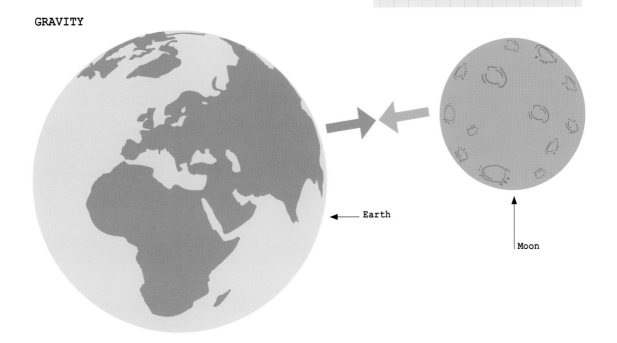

Earth

Moon

NAMING FORCES

There are lots of situations where a push comes from objects that are in contact, and engineers give them different names.

FRICTION is from objects rubbing together. It happens because their surfaces are bumpy on a microscopic level.

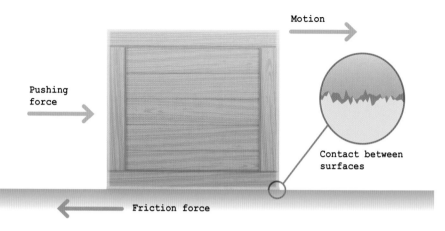

Motion

Pushing force

Contact between surfaces

Friction force

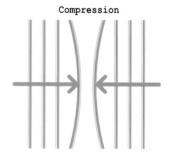

Compression

COMPRESSION is when an object is squeezed.

TENSION is when an object is stretched. When weight is put on a beam, there is compression on one side and tension on the other.

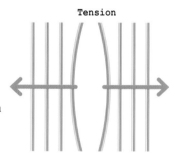

Tension

When you lean on a wall, the wall pushes you back. This kind of force is called a **NORMAL FORCE**.

Normal force

AIR RESISTANCE is the force on you as you move through air, from having to push the air out the way. The faster you move, the more resistance you feel.

Air resistance

BUOYANCY, or upthrust, is the force on anything that floats. Boats float because they weigh less than the water that is pushed out of the way.

THRUST is the forward push from an engine.

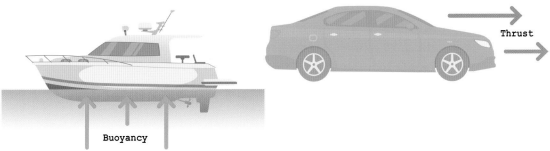

Buoyancy

Thrust

Balanced forces

If you were flying in deep space—without Earth's gravity, air resistance, or friction to slow you down—you would keep going straight ahead forever because there would be no forces on you. We rarely notice the Earth pulling down, the floor pushing up, or the atmosphere pushing on us from all sides, because all the forces push or pull against one another and balance out, making no overall force.

When a car moves at a constant speed, the forward thrust from the engine balances with the backward drag forces that come from air resistance and friction in the moving parts of the car. Cars have streamlined shapes to reduce drag, and need oil to reduce friction.

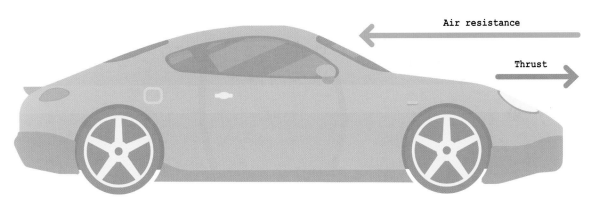

Air resistance

Thrust

Reaction forces

If you throw a heavy object forward, you will feel yourself being pushed backward by it. All forces come in pairs like this, and the pushback is called a reaction force. Reaction forces are always the same size as—and in the opposite direction to—the original force. This is how rockets work: as the fuel explodes, it turns into gases and expands. As it is pushed downward out of the rocket, the gas pushes up on the rocket and it takes off.

TINY BUILDING BLOCKS

Everything is made from tiny particles called atoms; there are about 10 trillion atoms in the ink in the dot above an i. Different substances get their properties from the way those atoms stick together and arrange themselves, and in a chemical reaction the atoms rearrange to make new substances. Roughly 60 million different substances have been discovered so far.

Atoms are tiny but are made from even smaller particles called protons, neutrons, and electrons. Protons and electrons push and pull on each other with electrostatic forces. The positive protons in the atom's nucleus attract the orbiting negative electrons. Objects with the same charge repel, so the electrons cannot get too close to one another and stay in orbits at different

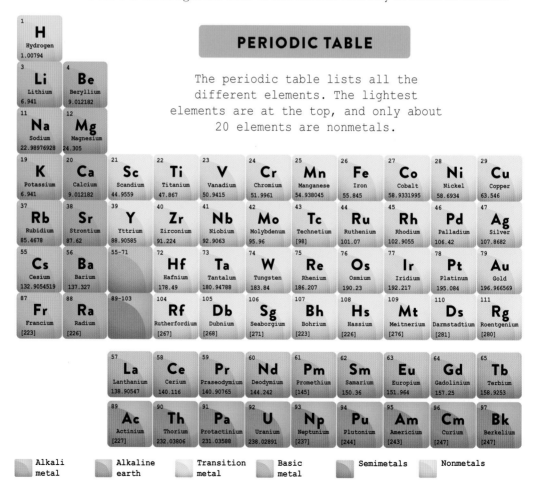

PERIODIC TABLE

The periodic table lists all the different elements. The lightest elements are at the top, and only about 20 elements are nonmetals.

ANATOMY OF AN ATOM

Even though almost all the mass of an atom is in its nucleus, the nucleus is actually tiny. If an atom was the size of a football stadium, the nucleus would be the size of a grape. This means that your body is mostly empty space.

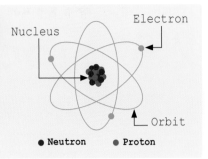

distances from the nucleus. Atoms with only one proton have an atomic number of one and all behave similarly. This is the element hydrogen, and all the different possible elements can be looked up on the periodic table, which arranges them by atomic number and by how they react. Some elements are common, like oxygen or iron, and others are only found in laboratories. In 2002, scientists created the biggest atom ever, oganesson, with 118 protons. Only five atoms have been detected since 2005.

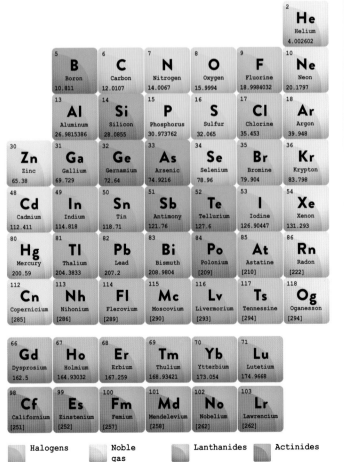

Halogens
Noble gas
Lanthanides
Actinides

ANSWER THIS

1. What causes atoms to rearrange themselves to form new substances?

2. What are atoms made from?

3. What is the charge of an electron?

4. Why do atoms stick to other atoms?

5. What is the name for the weak bonds between molecules?

Sticky atoms

Sometimes the outer electrons of an atom are attracted to the nucleus of another atom as well as its own, which causes atoms to stick together, or bond. They can bond very closely in particular shapes to form molecules or line up in repetitive patterns to form crystals, and the bonds are only broken and re-formed in chemical reactions.

Water molecules have one oxygen and two hydrogen atoms bonded tightly, but the molecules have weaker intermolecular bonds between them. Ice is formed when the molecules arrange themselves in a regular pattern. Heating can break intermolecular bonds, which is why substances melt.

WATER BONDS

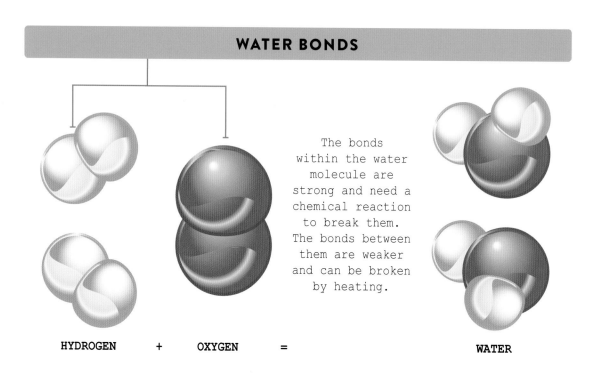

The bonds within the water molecule are strong and need a chemical reaction to break them. The bonds between them are weaker and can be broken by heating.

HYDROGEN   +   OXYGEN   =   WATER

FACT

If a carbon nanotube was rolled out flat, it would create a thin material called graphene. Graphene is the strongest material ever discovered. A 3.3-foot (1-meter) square sheet, just one atom thick, could support an 8.8-pound (4-kilogram) cat and weigh only as much as one of its whiskers. In practice, though, it is not possible to create a sheet this large.

Nanotechnology

Vantablack is the darkest paint ever created. It is so dark because the surface of it is made from a tiny forest of vertical tubes that are just a few atoms across. When light hits, it is trapped by the tubes and cannot reflect. Nanotechnology uses the interesting properties of structures that are made from a few hundred atoms, and can be used in a wide range of different things.

Carbon nanotubes, like those used for Vantablack, can be added to other substances to make them stronger, and are used to make wind turbines and baseball bats. Silver nanoparticles have been found to kill bacteria, and so bandages can be infused with them to help wounds heal faster.

CARBON NANOTUBES

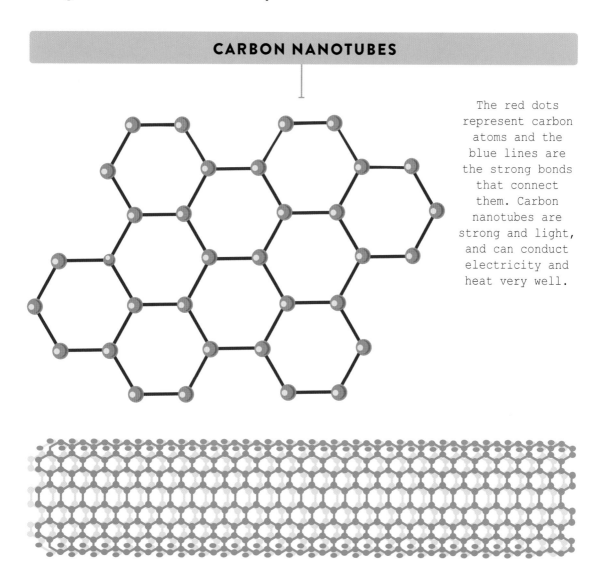

The red dots represent carbon atoms and the blue lines are the strong bonds that connect them. Carbon nanotubes are strong and light, and can conduct electricity and heat very well.

BALANCE OF ENERGY

LESSON 2.6

In the 1840s, Scottish brewer and scientist James Joule showed that the water at the bottom of a waterfall is very slightly warmer than at the top. He then showed how to calculate the increased motion of the water due to the fall, or the change in temperature for that much water, to get the same answer. This quantity is called energy, and its unit of measurement is the joule.

Since the number calculated before the change is the same as the number after, we say that energy is conserved in a change, meaning it cannot be created or destroyed, just moved between stores.

Storing and transfers

The water in a waterfall is pulled by gravity, so we can say that before the change, it was storing energy gravitationally. As it falls, it is pulled by gravity, and energy is transferred as it speeds up. Less and less energy is stored gravitationally as more is stored kinetically in the movement of the water. At the bottom of the waterfall, the water cannot flow as fast and the molecules push on one another, making them vibrate more. Molecules that vibrate faster are warmer, so the energy is now stored thermally in the water.

FACT

A bolt of lightning can transfer up to 10 billion joules of energy in about one thousandth of a second. That is enough to power an LED light bulb for more than three years.

ENERGY OF A WATERFALL

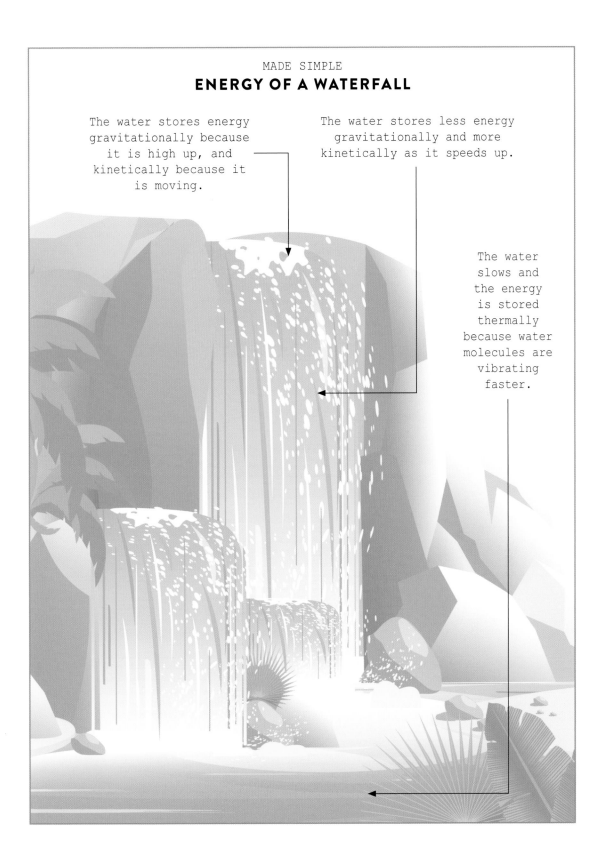

The water stores energy gravitationally because it is high up, and kinetically because it is moving.

The water stores less energy gravitationally and more kinetically as it speeds up.

The water slows and the energy is stored thermally because water molecules are vibrating faster.

ENERGY STORES

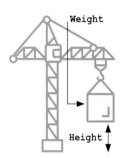

Weight

Height

GRAVITATIONAL

Gravitational stores depend on an object's weight and height. Cranes store energy in objects by lifting them.

Energy stored = weight (N) × height (m)

KINETIC

The kinetic store depends on the mass and speed of an object. Passenger jets store a lot of kinetic energy because they are heavy and fast.

Energy stored (J) = ½ × mass(kg) × speed² (m/s)

ELASTIC

The farther you stretch a spring or a bungee rope, the more energy it stores. Stiffer springs store more energy. Car suspension springs absorb energy from hitting bumps in the road.

THERMAL

The hotter something is compared to its surroundings, the more energy it stores. Thermal stores need insulation, or else the energy leaks out. Vacuum flasks keep that from happening.

MAGNETIC

If you make magnets stronger, they store more energy. Storing energy in magnets helps sort trash for recycling.

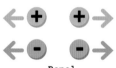

Repel

Attract

ELECTROSTATIC

When electrons move farther from the nucleus of the atom, they gain energy. Capacitors are electrical devices that can store energy in this way.

CHEMICAL

When you burn a fuel, the atoms react with the air and the reaction gives out energy. The fuel can be thought of as a store of energy. Batteries and food are chemical stores.

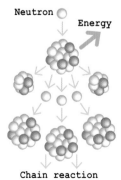

Neutron

Energy

Chain reaction

NUCLEAR

Sometimes the nuclei of atoms change, and they give out a lot of energy when they do. Nuclear power stations use the energy from these nuclear reactions to generate electricity.

ENERGY TRANSFERS

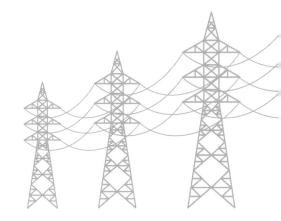

PUSHING AND PULLING

Pushing and pulling can be used to store energy in springs, lift things, or make things go faster. A crane lifts objects and transfers energy to a gravitational store.

LIGHTING

Only some of the light that can transfer energy is the energy you can see. Radio waves, microwaves, and X-rays transfer energy in a similar way but are invisible to our eyes.

ELECTRICITY

Electricity transfers energy by pushing electrons to make them flow through wires. It is a good way to transfer energy over long distances very quickly.

HEATING

This can happen through conduction, when hot atoms and molecules collide with cooler ones, which is how heat travels through the bottom of a saucepan. It can also happen through radiation, when hot objects emit infrared light waves. This is how bread toasts in a toaster.

Conduction — Convection — Radiation

ANSWER THIS

1. What is the unit of energy?

2. Why is the water warmer at the bottom of a waterfall than the top?

3. What is kinetic energy?

4. Name eight types of energy stores.

SCIENCE OF ENGINEERING

1. **How did ancient engineers know their building designs would be stable?**

   a. They used scientific laws

   b. They did experiments

   c. They had practical knowledge

   d. They read about previous designs in books

2. **Where was the first accurate way to calculate pi discovered?**

   a. India

   b. China

   c. Egypt

   d. Britain

3. **What were the first units of distance measurement based on?**

   a. The length of an animal

   b. The length of a body part

   c. The distance between two cities

   d. The length of a stick

4. **What is the name of the force that resists movement when two surfaces rub together?**

   a. Buoyancy

   b. Friction

   c. Normal force

   d. Thrust

5. **What two main forces determine how fast a vehicle can go?**

   a. Thrust and air resistance

   b. Weight and normal forces

   c. Thrust and buoyancy

   d. Weight and air resistance

6. **Roughly how many substances have ever been discovered?**

   a. 6,000

   b. 600,000

   c. 60 million

   d. 6 billion

7. **Why are silver nanoparticles added to bandages?**

   a. To make them shiny

   b. To make them water resistant

   c. They make skin grow faster

   d. They are antibacterial

8. **What is a water molecule made from?**

   a. Two oxygen atoms and one hydrogen atom

   b. One carbon atom and two oxygen atoms

   c. One carbon atom and two hydrogen atoms

   d. One oxygen atom and two hydrogen atoms

9. **Which of the following is a way to transfer energy?**

   a. Kinetic

   b. Electricity

   c. Thermal

   d. Gravitational

Answers on page 213

SIMPLE SUMMARY

Discovering the rules of nature is the job of scientists, who use experiments to test their ideas. Engineers can then use this knowledge to understand how their designs will work, and push technology to the limits of possibility.

• The idea of using experiments to test our understanding of nature first appeared in the writings of Ibn al-Haytham, who lived in Egypt at the turn of the 11th century, but it wasn't widely taken up until the 17th century.

• Numbers are used to find mathematical patterns and formulas that predict how engineered objects will work in the real world.

• Some of the biggest engineering projects are undertaken to build the experiments that probe the very smallest things we can measure.

• Forces that are twice as big accelerate objects twice as much, or objects that are twice as heavy, so a force is calculated by multiplying the mass and acceleration: Force (N) = mass (kg) $\times$ acceleration (m/s^2).

• Everything is made from tiny particles called atoms; different substances get their properties from the way those atoms stick together and arrange themselves, and in a chemical reaction the atoms rearrange to make new substances.

• Nanotechnology uses the interesting properties of structures that are made from a few hundred atoms.

• Energy is conserved in a change, meaning it cannot be created or destroyed, just moved between stores.

3

BUILDING STRUCTURES

For thousands of years, humans have been engineering structures that provide protection from the elements, keeping us safe and warm. At its simplest, designing a structure means understanding the forces that help keep objects from collapsing. Engineering more complex buildings today means finding light, strong materials that are environmentally friendly, and putting them together in efficient ways so they can reach for the sky . . . and beyond.

WHAT YOU WILL LEARN

Ancient construction

Sky's the limit

Building bridges

Digging deep

Living on another world

ANCIENT CONSTRUCTION

Nobody knows when or how human ancestors began to construct shelters, rather than just make use of what nature provided. It's likely that the earliest forms of construction would have been made from materials that have long degraded. But we do know that by 10,000 BC, people were investing time and effort in building durable structures made from large blocks of stone.

Remains of one of the oldest architectural structures in the world can be found at the Paleolithic site of Göbekli Tepe in Turkey. Dated to around 9000 BC, the blocks are thought to have once formed a temple where people gathered to worship. This suggests that long before people made houses from stone, they built monuments for religious ceremonies. It's thought that as groups of people collected food in the form of crops and livestock, they would have settled permanently near these sites. This new culture of farming, the Neolithic revolution, allowed people to spend time developing bigger, more elaborate buildings.

FACT

Traces of the oldest surviving example of human architecture can still be seen in the Barwon River in Australia. The structures could be more than 40,000 years old, which would make them a truly ancient example of human ingenuity. Built by ancient Aboriginal people to catch fish swimming upstream, it's believed that communities would gather from all around to feast at the site.

BUILDING STONEHENGE

England's Stonehenge, built in stages 4,000-5,000 years ago, is one of the most famous Bronze Age structures. Its larger stones are made of sandstone dragged from a site more than 18 miles (30 kilometers) away. They were carved using hard "hammer stones," with specially carved joints that locked them in place.

Stacking stones

Most surviving examples of ancient construction are of carved blocks of stone stacked in ways that make it hard for them to fall down. Pyramids and ziggurats (massive terraced structures) are famous examples of stacked blocks that have stood the test of time. They were permanent structures, often built as memorials and tombs.

An important innovation for creating blocks that can be stacked was the development of harder metals. Early metal tools were made from copper, which was easy to extract from ore called malachite, but was too soft to efficiently cut harder rocks such as granite.

Around 5,000 years ago, people found ways to mix tin with copper to form the alloy bronze, which was harder than copper. Iron was harder still—smelting iron ore led to a new age in technology and construction, in which more durable construction materials could be carved with precision.

> ### ANSWER THIS
>
> 1. What was the structure built at Göbekli Tepe in Turkey around 9000 BC probably used for?
>
> 2. What helped people invest more time and effort in building larger, more durable structures?
>
> 3. What was the purpose of most ancient pyramids and ziggurats?
>
> 4. How old are the fish traps in Australia's Barwon River thought to be?
>
> 5. What are the larger stones in England's Stonehenge made from?

3.2 SKY'S THE LIMIT

As anybody who has tried to stack blocks to the ceiling would know, every extra block makes it wobble a little more, until it tips . . . and falls. That means the tallest buildings for thousands of years, such as pyramids and ziggurats, were built like hills with wide bases.

Some of the first attempts to build ever higher were done for religious reasons, constructing huge cathedrals that felt majestic and powerful. To avoid the need to use a mountain of stone, architects devised ways to spread forces cleverly with angled supports called buttresses. Still, the insides of these cavernous buildings were dark and gloomy. Large windows would make the heavy walls less stable, so any gaps needed to be small and narrow.

By the Middle Ages, engineers found they could use even less stone by including arches that spread the load horizontally, rather than letting it pile up below. Buttresses were slimmed down, giving them a slim look that earned them the name "flying buttresses." Windows were made with rounded or slightly pointed tops, so they were strong enough to be increased in size.

A home among the clouds

In the 19th century, the Industrial Revolution brought more people to the cities, creating a demand for more housing and offices. Building up was the only option, but there was little room for big buttresses—and nobody wanted to climb 10 flights of stairs every day.

FACT

For nearly 4,000 years, the Great Pyramid of Giza in Cairo, Egypt, was the tallest structure in the world. At just over 479 feet (146 meters), it was a record that remained unbroken until Lincoln Cathedral, England, received a new central tower in 1311. The tower and its spire reached 525 feet (160 meters) above the ground.

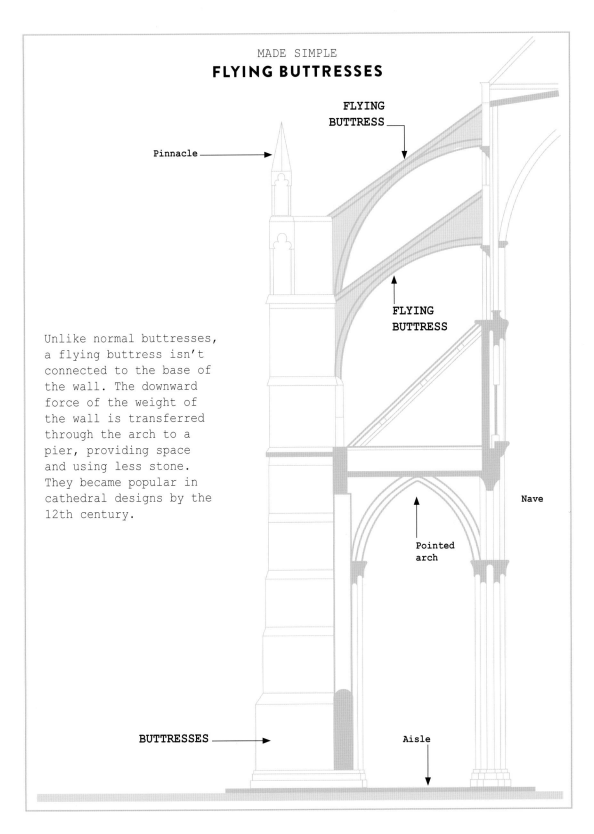

MADE SIMPLE
FLYING BUTTRESSES

FLYING BUTTRESS

Pinnacle

FLYING BUTTRESS

Unlike normal buttresses, a flying buttress isn't connected to the base of the wall. The downward force of the weight of the wall is transferred through the arch to a pier, providing space and using less stone. They became popular in cathedral designs by the 12th century.

Nave

Pointed arch

BUTTRESSES

Aisle

MADE SIMPLE
HOW TRACTION ELEVATORS WORK

Sheave: A grooved drum that works like a large pulley

Electric motor: Powers the sheave, lifting and lowering the car

Car: A compartment that protects the cargo being lifted; often guided by grooved rails that catch the car if the cables break

Cables: Usually made from strands of steel woven in together

Counterweight: Weighs the same as a car that's just less than half full; its purpose is to provide a balance for the pulley, making the motor spend less energy raising it

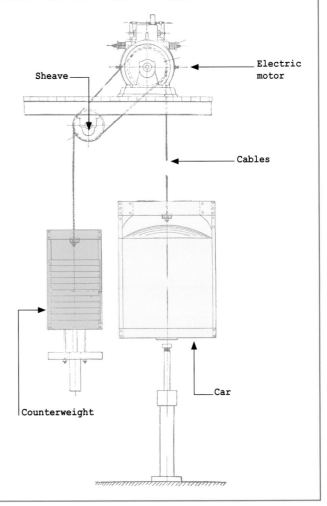

Sheave

Electric motor

Cables

Counterweight

Car

Buttresses wouldn't help in these crowded conditions, so taller buildings needed to be supported with something other than stone. Improvements in the way beams were made meant buildings could be based on steel skeletons with big glass windows and thin stone walls.

The first true skyscrapers only became possible with the invention of powered elevators in the middle of the 19th century. An American inventor named Elisha Otis wasn't the first to come up with a way to lift materials between floors, but he did add a safety catch that meant people trusted them enough to take a ride.

Tall buildings can be the perfect spot for lightning to strike over and over again. In 1749, the American statesman Benjamin Franklin first noted a way to protect tall structures from damage caused by lightning. The lightning rod is a conductive material that safely carries the charge into the ground.

Tallest of the tall

In 2009 the Burj Khalifa in Dubai became the tallest building ever to be constructed, stretching an astonishing 2,723 feet (830 meters) above the surface from the base to the very top and containing 163 floors. It's an impressive feat of engineering and design that had to overcome a number of challenges.

Building a tower a couple of thousand feet in height requires rather large buttresses, even with a steel scaffold. So the Burj Khalifa uses just three narrow buttress wings, providing the right balance of less material for the best support, while still providing those inside with plenty of windows to look through.

Then there's the problem of access: nobody would want to climb 163 floors in a staircase, and waiting for an elevator to visit hundreds of floors is nearly as bad, even if it is moving quickly. Having a variety of express elevators that only service some floors is necessary in super-tall skyscrapers. As buildings reach ever higher, those trips could get longer and longer. What's more, in emergencies, elevators become too risky to use. If a fire breaks out on a top floor, for instance, descending all of those steps would become increasingly perilous.

One last problem to overcome is the effect wind has on large buildings. Like a large sail, the sides of skyscrapers can catch moving air, causing them to sway dangerously. To avoid this, the Burj Khalifa has a special tapering shape that deflects air currents rather than catching them.

ANSWER THIS

1. What special, lightweight structure did medieval engineers design to hold up the walls of cathedrals?

2. How tall is the Burj Khalifa in Dubai?

3. What are two engineering challenges tall buildings needed to overcome?

4. For how long was the Great Pyramid of Giza the world's tallest construction?

3.3 BUILDING BRIDGES

If you stand on a short wooden plank covering a narrow stream, gravity pulls your center of mass downward. Newton's laws tell us the plank resists with an equal, upward force, which in turn is transferred down the plank and into the ground at either end.

Like most structures, bridges must be designed to deal with two mechanical forces called tension and compression. Tension is a pulling force, like the stretching of rope in a tug-of-war. Compression is a squeezing force, like in the crunching of a carrot as you bite down on it. This downward force being transferred through the plank causes some of the wood to compress and other parts to experience tension. If the force is too great—maybe because the mass is too heavy, or the distance between the banks is too far—the wood will either snap apart or crumble together, breaking the bridge.

To make bridges that don't break apart the moment you step on them, those forces need to be distributed through the bridge or transferred. The following pages show a few ways engineers can manage that.

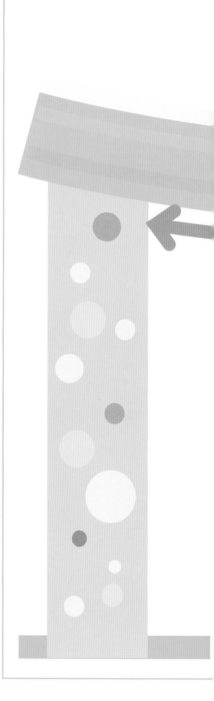

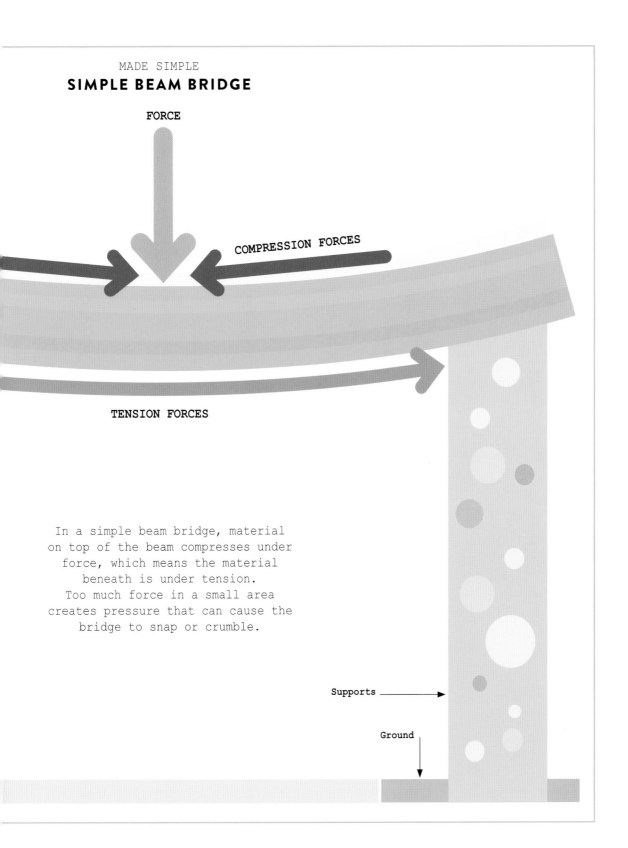

SIMPLE BEAM BRIDGE

FORCE

COMPRESSION FORCES

TENSION FORCES

In a simple beam bridge, material on top of the beam compresses under force, which means the material beneath is under tension.
Too much force in a small area creates pressure that can cause the bridge to snap or crumble.

Supports

Ground

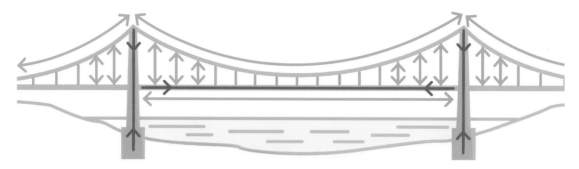

SUSPENSION BRIDGES

These bridges use long cables to transfer forces on the bridge to pillars at either end. The cables are designed to cope with large amounts of tension. The short pillars in suspension bridges are designed to deal with high amounts of compression.
Example: Golden Gate Bridge, San Francisco.

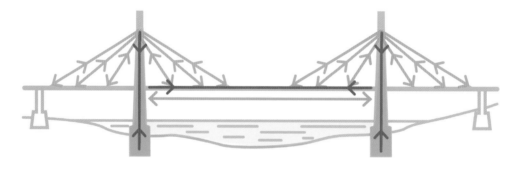

CABLE-STAYED BRIDGES

Some bridges use shorter cables to transfer forces directly into pillars. These cable-stayed bridges are lighter than other suspension bridges, but need taller pillars.
Example: Millau Viaduct, France.

FACT

The London Millennium Footbridge over the river Thames caused controversy when it opened in the year 2000. Bridges are designed to handle tiny wobbles, but something called resonance made this one worse. Just as a swing goes higher with each well-timed push, the combined steps of crowds of people walking across the bridge added enough pushes at the right time to make it sway. After some reengineering, the bridge reopened in 2002, wobble-free.

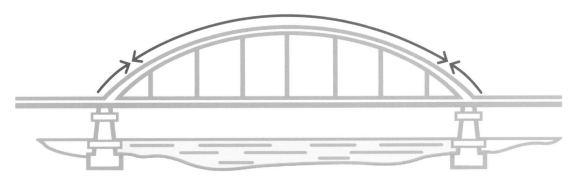

ARCHED BRIDGES

Arched bridges use arches to transfer forces into supportive structures at the end called abutments. These bridges work by distributing a force into a horizontal thrust that pushes outward against the abutments. Example: Sydney Harbour Bridge, Australia.

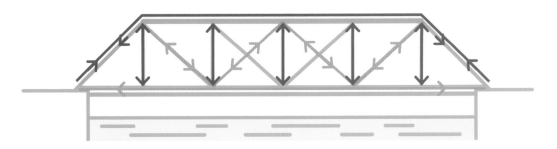

TRUSS BRIDGES

Other bridges use triangular structures called trusses to spread tension and compression without adding a lot of mass. Truss bridges are simple and don't need pillars or abutments at either end.
Example: Kapellbrücke, Switzerland.

KEY
→ Compression
→ Tension

ANSWER THIS

1. What is a compression force?

2. What is a tension force?

3. Which bridge type transfers forces into short pillars at the ends of a bridge through long cables?

4. Which bridge type transfers forces into abutments by turning a downward force into a horizontal force?

5. Why did the Millennium Footbridge in London wobble when it first opened?

3.4 DIGGING DEEP

As simple as it might seem, tunneling a passage beneath the earth's surface can be a challenge for engineers. Some materials, such as sand, don't hold their shape well. Others, like granite, are extremely hard to dig through. Sometimes there are pockets of water that seep in, flooding the cavity. Then there is the air supply to consider—even if you have plenty, toxic gases like methane can pose problems.

FACT

At just over 31 miles (50 kilometers) in length, the Channel Tunnel is certainly long. While it's not the longest tunnel in the world, it does have the longest section underwater, with nearly 24 miles (38 kilometers) running more than 328 feet (100 meters) below the channel's surface.

The deepest hole ever dug into the earth's surface is part of a complex of shafts on the Kola Peninsula in northwest Russia. While the deepest shaft is more than 7.5 miles (12.2 kilometers) deep), it's also only about 9 inches (23 centimeters) in width.

MADE SIMPLE
BRUNEL'S SHIELD

B

Marc Isambard Brunel's shield **(A)** helped build the world's first underwater tunnel, connecting the sides of the river Thames. It protected workers as they dug out material **(B)** by using boards held into place **(C)**. The whole shield could be moved forward **(D)** bit by bit as the tunnel was lengthened.

Engineers rely on geologists analyzing an area by drilling boreholes or using sonar technology. This tells them about the types of rock underground, where the water table is, and whether there is a geological fault or crack. Once a path for a tunnel has been determined, excavation can begin.

> **ANSWER THIS**

1. What are three challenges in digging tunnels?

2. What is Marc Isambard Brunel's tunneling shield?

3. How many boring machines were made to dig the Channel Tunnel?

4. What year did the two sides of the Channel Tunnel meet?

5. How deep is the deepest human-dug shaft?

There are a number of ways tunnels can be carved out of the ground. One is called cut-and-cover—a trench is dug into the ground, and then covered over with a roof. These are good for simple, shallow tunnels. Another method is using a tunneling shield. Designed by the English engineer Marc Isambard Brunel in the early 19th century, it was originally an iron wall with several levels for workers to excavate material in safety, shuffling forward when each new section of tunnel was well supported.

The shape of the cross-section is important. Many tunnels have a circular cross-section because circles distribute forces evenly around their circumference. Rectangular cross-sections concentrate forces, creating stress points where the force of squeezed rock can cause the tunnel to fail.

Channel + tunnel = Chunnel

Tunnels are usually built where it's too long or too troublesome to build a bridge. Connecting England with France by digging a long tunnel was finally made possible in 1988 by the development of a massive "tunnel boring machine." A total of 11 of these machines were made, each hundreds of feet in length. The project succeeded in 1990, when the tunnels being mined under the channel connected together. It would be another four years, though, before the "Chunnel" was formally opened.

LIVING ON ANOTHER WORLD

The Moon isn't a nice place to live. Sure, the view is amazing. But the dust particles are tiny enough to get into just about every crack. Without wind or water to wear them down, they're sharp and abrasive. And they're charged, so they cling to everything.

Then there's the extreme temperatures to deal with. And intense radiation. And low gravity. So building a place to live in on the Moon would need a lot of clever engineering using readily available materials that don't need to be carried up on expensive rockets.

The first thing that Moon accommodation would need is protection from tiny meteorites zooming down at speeds up to 45 miles (72 kilometers) per second, and the constant stream of radiation. One solution is to build tiny rooms and cover them with a thick layer of moondust and rock called "regolith." Another is to build inside the hollow remains of ancient lava tubes. In 2017, American and Japanese researchers used radar images to spot a potential sub-lunar cavity for hiding a whole city on the near side of the Moon. Deep under the surface, it would be safe from most radiation and small meteorites.

Printing houses

The Moon would be a short jump next door compared to the arduous seven-month trip to get to Mars using current technologies. That's a lot of time and a lot of fuel, so carrying even some sturdy tents for early colonists would be expensive.

Engineers are hoping to solve this by sending up some giant 3-D printers long before humans arrive. On Earth, it's already a possibility, but to do this on Mars, machinery would need to make clever use of the sand and rocks in the environment. NASA has already held competitions for ideas. One possibility is to use water from ice and calcium oxide, and mix it with material from the surface to make a Martian concrete. Another, called MARSHA, is to bond local materials with a kind of robust plastic glue that doesn't flex too much with temperature changes. However engineers manage it, structures on Mars will need to be pressurized, warm, and have plenty of room. After all, those first colonists will be stuck up there for a while—they're going to need space away from their roommates.

In the 1990s, scientists conducted experiments inside a facility called Biosphere 2 to see if humans could live inside a perfectly sealed, ecologically balanced system for long periods. The subjects experienced a multitude of problems that proved how challenging it would be on another world.

MADE SIMPLE
THE PROTON CHALLENGE

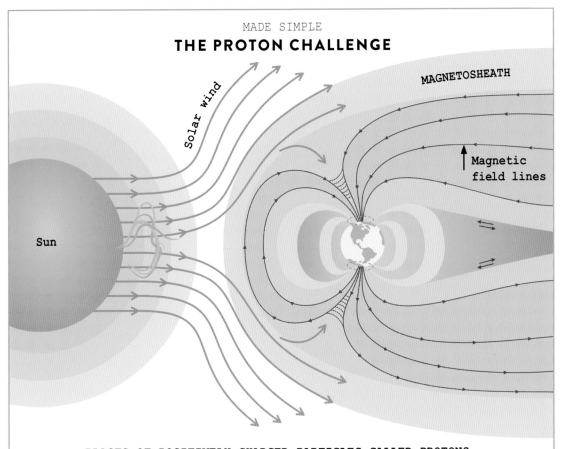

Solar wind

MAGNETOSHEATH

Magnetic field lines

Sun

BLASTS OF POSITIVELY CHARGED PARTICLES CALLED PROTONS make up most of the concerning radiation that colonists of the Moon and Mars would need to deal with. On Earth, most of these are deflected by our planet's magnetic field. To protect Martian and lunar visitors from storms of these particles, future engineers might use thick layers of rock, tanks of water, or dense lead shields to create rooms, or a room-sized magnetic field.

BUILDINGS

1. When did humans first build permanent settlements using large stones as durable building materials? About:

a. 100,000 years ago

b. 10,000 years ago

c. 2,000 years ago

d. 1 million years ago

2. Which material formed the basis of early metal tools?

a. Bone

b. Gold

c. Copper

d. Tungsten

3. Which ancient buildings were the tallest structures for thousands of years?

a. Pyramids and ziggurats

b. Skyscrapers

c. Castles

d. Churches

4. Which direction do arches transfer force from load?

a. Straight down

b. Straight up

c. Both up and down

d. Horizontally

5. Where did large numbers of people migrate to during the Industrial Revolution?

a. The cities

b. The country

c. The seaside

d. The mountains

6. Which material led to stronger "skeletons" for modern tall buildings?

a. Glass

b. Marble

c. Steel

d. Wood

7. What describes the two primary forces in bridges?

a. Compression and centrifugal

b. Gravitational and tension

c. Gravitational and centrifugal

d. Compression and tension

8. Which technological advancement helped make the long-anticipated Channel Tunnel possible?

a. Tunnel boring machines

b. Tube drilling devices

c. Tough biting metals

d. Hole digging engines

9. In 2017, a lava tube was spotted on the Moon. It was big enough to protect:

a. A single human

b. A small building

c. A small town

d. A whole lunar city

Answers on page 213

SIMPLE SUMMARY

Designing a structure means understanding the forces that help keep objects from collapsing. Engineering more complex buildings means finding light, strong materials that are environmentally friendly, and putting them together in efficient ways.

• Remains of one of the oldest architectural structures in the world can be found at the Paleolithic site of Göbekli Tepe in Turkey.

• To avoid the need to use a mountain of stone, architects devised ways to spread forces cleverly with angled supports called buttresses. The slimmed-down buttresses of the Middle Ages were called "flying buttresses."

• The first true skyscrapers became possible only with the invention of powered elevators in the middle of the 19th century.

• In 2009 the Burj Khalifa in Dubai became the tallest building ever to be constructed, stretching 2,723 feet (830 meters) above the surface from the base to the top and containing 163 floors.

• Bridges must be designed to deal with two mechanical forces called tension and compression.

• Connecting England with France by digging a long tunnel was finally made possible in 1988, by the development of a massive tunnel boring machine.

• Blasts of positively charged particles called protons make up most of the concerning radiation that colonists of the Moon and Mars would need to deal with.

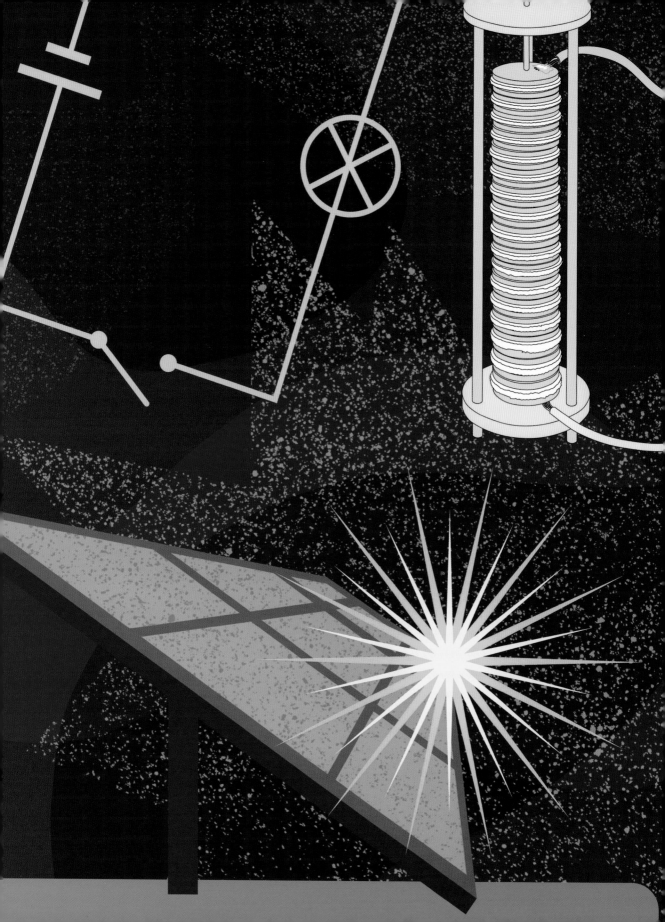

4

POWER AND ENGINEERING

Humans get their energy from the food we eat, but we are limited by how much our bodies can store and use at once. Around 100,000 years ago, we learned to control fire to release the energy stored chemically in wood to get more nutrients from our food and to live in colder climates.

WHAT YOU WILL LEARN

Energy sources

Electricity

Generating electricity

Powering nations

Going green

4.1 ENERGY SOURCES

Energy is stored everywhere, but not all of it can be made usable. The molecules of air that surround us are moving at an average speed of almost 1,000 miles per hour (about 1,600 kilometers per hour), but to capture the energy of their tiny random motions is hard. When the wind blows, air molecules move together in one direction and can be used to push something. Energy sources are stores of energy, like the wind, that can be made to transfer their energy in a useful way.

When plants photosynthesize, they store energy chemically in their cells. This energy can then be released in a useful way by burning it. Wood was the first energy source for humans over 100,000 years ago and is still used today.

When living things die, their stored energy is usually used by the microorganisms that break it down, which is why compost heaps sometimes feel warm. However, if living matter gets buried, the lack of oxygen means it will not decompose. If buried deep underground for millions of years, the heat and pressure in the Earth's crust can turn it into coal, oil, or natural gas. Most of the world's energy comes from these fossil fuels because they are cheap, easy to transport, and release a lot of energy very quickly when burned. We call these fuels nonrenewable because once they have been burned they are gone forever.

ANSWER THIS

1. What is a nonrenewable energy source?

2. What was the first fuel used by humans?

3. How does a fossil fuel form?

4. When and where were the first windmills built?

5. List four sources of energy that do not rely on the Sun.

Go with the flow

Moving fluids like the wind and rivers can transfer their kinetic stores by pushing a sail or a turbine. Waterwheels have been used to capture the kinetic energy of rivers since they were first invented in the Middle East in the fourth or third century BC. Wind has also been used for thousands of years to push boats, and the first windmills were invented in Persia during the ninth century. They were used to pump water or to grind grain. These are both considered renewable energy because rivers and wind will not disappear when their energy is captured.

Energy without the Sun

Fossil fuels and plants absorbed energy from the Sun through photosynthesis. The wind's energy also comes from the Sun, as it is caused by uneven heating of the atmosphere. Even rivers get their energy from the Sun since they are formed when water in the air, which was evaporated by the Sun, condenses at the tops of mountains and hills.

If we did not have the Sun, though, we would still be able to harness energy. Batteries use chemical reactions to transfer energy by electricity, nuclear reactions release a lot of heat, and in some places the Earth's crust is thin enough that we can use the geothermal heat from the Earth's core to heat water. While the Sun is partly responsible, the Moon's gravitational pull causes the tides, which can also be used to capture energy.

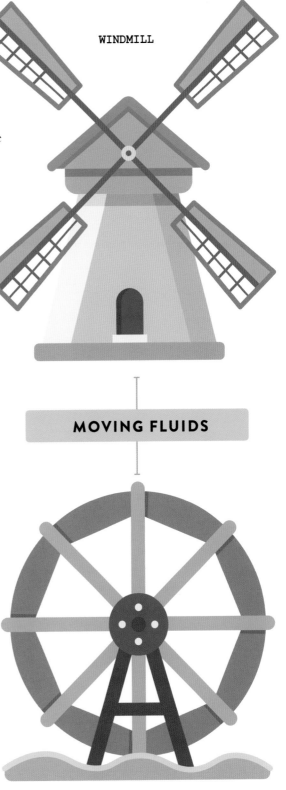

WINDMILL

MOVING FLUIDS

WATERWHEEL

Commonly used energy sources

These commonly used energy sources all have advantages and disadvantages compared to one another, but renewable sources are becoming more important as the effects of burning fossil fuels on the climate become more extreme.

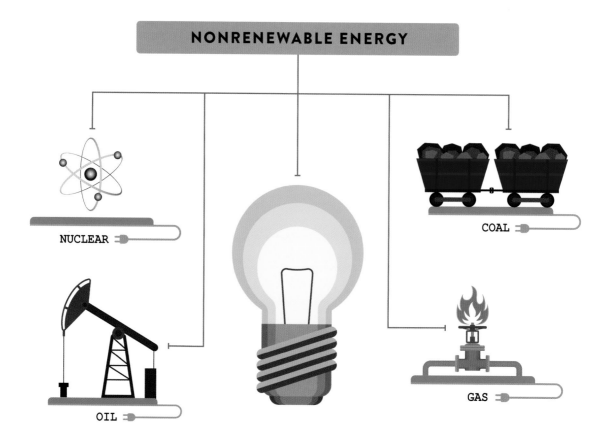

NONRENEWABLE ENERGY

NUCLEAR

OIL

COAL

GAS

Nuclear: Nuclear power is very efficient, with an entire lifetime's energy needs supplied by a piece of uranium the size of an egg, but it also produces radioactive waste.

Oil: Formed from the burial of ancient sea life, oil can be separated into different fuels. Some is burned in power stations, but others (like gasoline) provide energy for transportation.

Coal: Formed by the burial of ancient forests, coal is cheap and easy to transport, but it creates a lot of pollution.

Gas: Gas produces the least pollution of the fossil fuels and the amount being burned can be easily controlled, making it more efficient, but it still contributes to global warming.

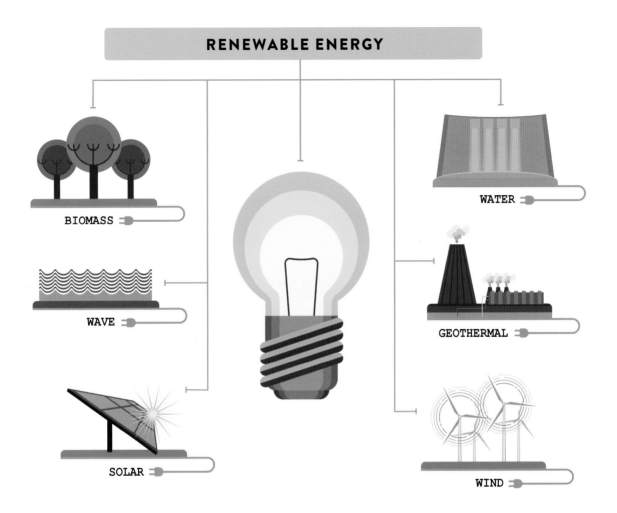

RENEWABLE ENERGY

BIOMASS

WAVE

SOLAR

WATER

GEOTHERMAL

WIND

Biomass: Wood and vegetable oils are examples of biomass. They are renewable, as it is easy to grow more.

Wave: Wave power uses floating objects that generate electricity as they are moved by the waves.

Solar: Solar panels can be used to generate electricity or warm water as they absorb energy directly from the Sun.

Water: By building a dam in a river, hydroelectric power stations capture the movement of water by letting it turn turbines as it flows through.

Geothermal: Radioactive elements in the Earth's core mean that it is always hot. Where the Earth's crust is thin, the steam from hot underground water can be used to turn turbines.

Wind: Huge turbines are turned by the wind. Many wind turbines are put out at sea where they are out of the way and where there is more wind.

4.2 ELECTRICITY

Flowing electricity (or current) and electrostatic forces are caused by the attraction and repulsion due to charge, which is a property of the electrons and protons that make up atoms. It is now the most efficient and convenient way to transfer energy to homes and businesses, powering our machines and providing the heat and light that we rely on every day.

The ancient Egyptians were the first to write about flowing electricity when describing the shock of the electric eel. The ancient Greeks also described electrical forces when they noticed that amber rubbed with fur could attract light objects such as feathers. The first reliable way to produce an electric current came in 1800 when Alessandro Volta created the voltaic pile, which was like a battery made from copper (Cu) and zinc (Zn) disks, separated by paper soaked in saltwater (NaCl is sodium chloride, or salt, and H_2O is water). Soon it was discovered that flowing electricity caused magnetic fields, and in 1821 Michael Faraday used magnets to invent the first electric motor.

FACT

Different circuits require different voltages depending on the components inside or the amount of energy that needs to be transferred. A phone charger produces 5V, an electric car has up to 400V, and the electricity in power cables can have hundreds of thousands of volts. Lightning has a much higher voltage, in the tens of millions of volts.

A VOLTAIC PILE

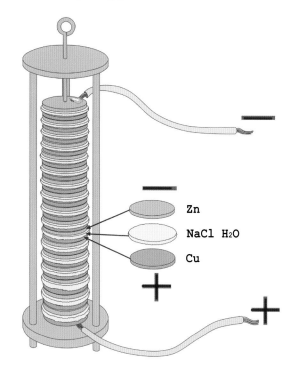

Zn

NaCl H_2O

Cu

By the end of the 19th century, engineers had used electricity for instant communications, with the invention of the telegraph and telephone; elsewhere, Thomas Edison's generator built in the 1870s allowed electricity to be generated on an industrial scale to power trains and lighting. Before electric lighting, people burned fuels for light, which was more expensive, less bright, and carried a high risk of starting fires. At the end of the 19th century, Heinrich Hertz discovered that electricity could also be used to make radio waves. These advances opened up a wealth of possibilities for engineers and made the modern world possible.

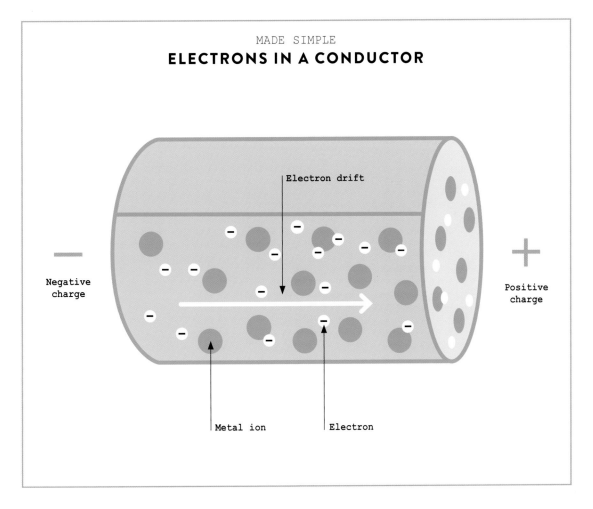

MADE SIMPLE

ELECTRONS IN A CONDUCTOR

Electron drift

Negative charge

Positive charge

Metal ion   Electron

Conductors and circuits

The electrons on the outside of atoms in a metal wire are able to leave the atoms and move around between them. Since they are negatively charged, they can be pushed around by other charged objects and made to flow like water flowing through a river.

Rivers can have large currents by being wide or by flowing faster, and electrons in wires are the same. Wider wires have more electrons that can flow, but you can make them flow faster by giving them a bigger push too. The push behind an electrical current is called its voltage, and anything that allows charge to pass through it, like a metal, is called a conductor.

There are two ways that charge can flow through a wire. In a direct current, which is what you might get from a battery, the charge flows continuously around a circuit, but in an alternating current, which is used for the mains, the charge moves backward and forward. For both types of currents, there needs to be a complete circuit of conductors between each side of the power source for electricity to flow.

Electrical components, like resistors or diodes, can be built into circuits to change the current. Other components can transfer the energy of the current to something useful, like a motor or a light bulb. Electrical engineers use circuit diagrams with symbols for components to design circuits, as they are clear to read.

> ### ANSWER THIS
>
> 1. What is the force that causes electricity?
>
> 2. What is a voltaic pile?
>
> 3. What are the charged particles that move through a wire to form an electric current?
>
> 4. What is an alternating current?
>
> 5. Why do electrical engineers use circuit diagrams to design circuits?

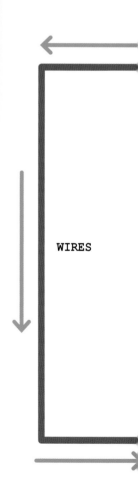

WIRES

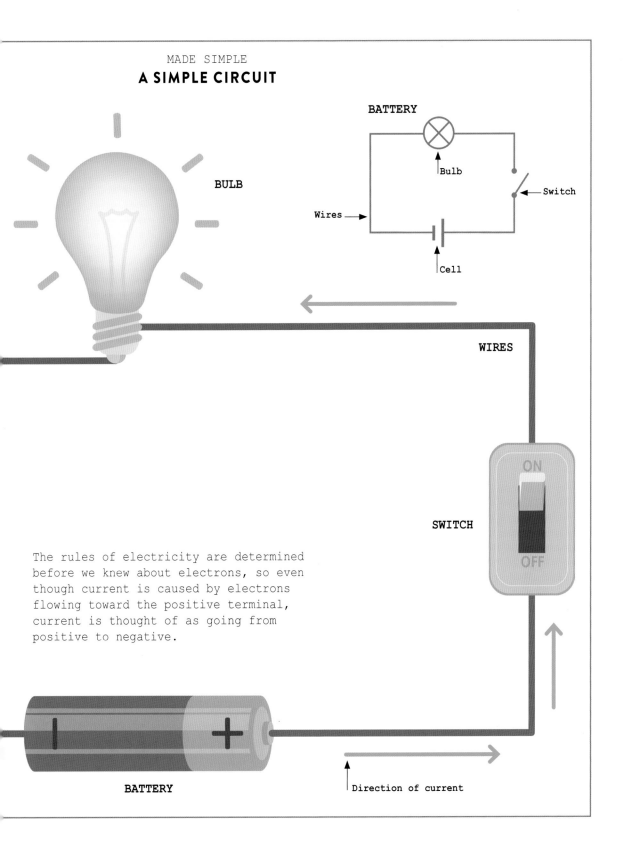

MADE SIMPLE

A SIMPLE CIRCUIT

BULB

BATTERY

Bulb

Switch

Wires →

Cell

WIRES

SWITCH

ON

OFF

The rules of electricity are determined before we knew about electrons, so even though current is caused by electrons flowing toward the positive terminal, current is thought of as going from positive to negative.

BATTERY

Direction of current

GENERATING ELECTRICITY

There are a number of ways that engineers can make electric current flow. Batteries use chemical reactions but cannot transfer energy very quickly, making them suitable for smaller, portable machines. To make large currents with which to supply homes and industry, generators are needed. Solar cells produce an electric current when hit by light, and piezoelectric materials can even generate electricity from being stretched or squashed, giving a range of ways for engineers to capture energy and transfer it to our machines.

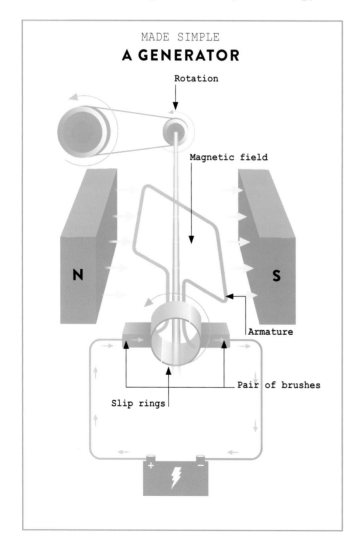

MADE SIMPLE
A GENERATOR

Rotation

Magnetic field

N

S

Armature

Slip rings

Pair of brushes

In 1831, Michael Faraday demonstrated that moving a wire at right angles to a magnetic field produces a current in the wire. As the wire moves, the electrons inside move with it and create their own magnetic field. This interacts with the magnetic field from the magnet to push the electrons through the wire.

By making the wire into a coil, moving it faster, and increasing the magnetic field, the effect is increased.

Cells
Inside an electric cell a substance called an electrolyte is in contact with two different conductors called electrodes. One of the electrodes, the anode, reacts with the electrolyte to produce spare electrons, making it negatively charged. The other conductor reacts to take in electrons, making it positively charged.

MADE SIMPLE
INSIDE A DRY CELL BATTERY

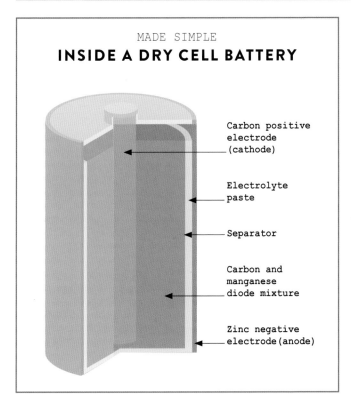

Carbon positive electrode (cathode)

Electrolyte paste

Separator

Carbon and manganese diode mixture

Zinc negative electrode (anode)

ANSWER THIS

1. Who invented the first electric generator?

2. Why does a generator need magnets?

3. How can a generator be made to produce a larger current?

4. What is a battery?

5. What is piezoelectricity?

However, since the electrodes are separated from each other within the cell, the reaction cannot take place unless they are attached by conductors in a circuit. If you attach two or more cells together, it is called a battery.

Solar cells

In 1958, the *Vanguard 1* satellite was launched by NASA. It was the first machine to be powered by light using solar panels, which are groups of solar cells attached together. Solar cells are made with the semiconducting material silicon. Normally, silicon atoms will not allow their electrons to flow, but when light hits them, electrons can jump out of the atoms and create a current. As long as there is enough light, they are a great source of renewable energy.

4.4 POWERING NATIONS

In 2018, the world generated enough electricity for every person on Earth to have a TV, a laptop, and four bright light bulbs running continuously. In order to generate that much energy, power stations all over the globe work night and day, and to get the electrical power to people's homes, they are all connected by large networks of pylons and wires. If electrical power is not used, the energy is wasted by heating up the wires, so engineers are always looking for ways to power nations more efficiently.

Power stations contain generators that need to be turned to generate electricity. Some use the energy released from burning fuels or nuclear reactions to boil water. The steam produced pushes turbines, which turn the generators, producing large currents.

Large currents heat up wires, and the longer the wires, the more they heat up, so transferring electricity over long distances is inefficient. The invention of the transformer in 1885 solved this problem by allowing the same power to be distributed with smaller currents.

FACT

The first public electricity supply was developed in 1881 in the small English town of Godalming. They used hydroelectricity by using a waterwheel in the local river, but the system had many problems and was shut down by 1884. They did not have electricity for another 20 years.

FROM THE POWER STATION TO THE HOME

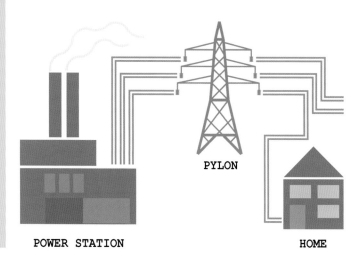

PYLON

POWER STATION

HOME

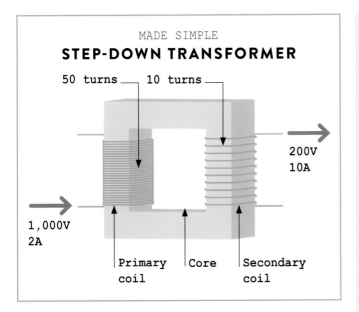

MADE SIMPLE
STEP-DOWN TRANSFORMER

50 turns — 10 turns

200V
10A

1,000V
2A

Primary coil Core Secondary coil

ANSWER THIS

1. What is fuel used for in a power station?

2. What happens to long wires when an electric current goes through them?

3. What is the job of a step-up transformer?

4. What is the job of a step-down transformer?

5. At what point in a 24 hour period will electricity use be lowest?

Transformers have a coil of wire with an alternating current going through, wound around an iron core. The current creates a magnetic field in the core, which then creates a current in a second coil of wire. If the second coil has more turns, then the current will be lower but the voltage will be higher and the same energy is transferred. This type of transformer is called a step-up transformer, and power stations use them before distributing electricity across the country. Very high voltages are dangerous, though, so step-down transformers, which have fewer turns on the second coil, are placed near homes to reduce the voltage before the electricity is used.

Avoiding wasted energy

Any unused electricity simply heats up wires and the energy is lost, so engineers monitor the patterns of energy usage to help them know how much to generate at any one time. At night, most people are asleep and not using much energy, so power stations burn less fuel. When everyone wakes up in the morning, turning on their lights and appliances, the demand goes up. In the evening, when it gets dark, demand can go up further when more lights are turned on. There are also seasonal changes in demand, since more electric heaters and lights are used in winter.

4.5 GOING GREEN

By the 1950s, scientists noticed that our atmosphere was warming, mainly due to an increase in carbon dioxide from the burning of fossil fuels. Since then, energy needs have become much greater and there is now two and a half times as much carbon dioxide in the atmosphere than there was 250 years ago.

Burning fuels leads to other problems, too. The waste gases released can react with the water in the air to make the rain more acidic, which is bad for plants and lakes, and this air can also cause health problems when breathed in. A big challenge facing today's engineers is to find ways to meet our energy needs without damaging our health and the health of the plants and animals on which we rely for survival.

Green energy

Renewables, such as hydroelectric and tidal power, are limited by where power stations can be built. Wind power is the cheapest, most efficient way to generate energy, but we cannot rely on the wind to blow, and solar power can only be relied on when there is enough sunlight. The solution for unpredictable sources of energy is to have a way to store it when it is not in demand so that it can be released at times of high demand.

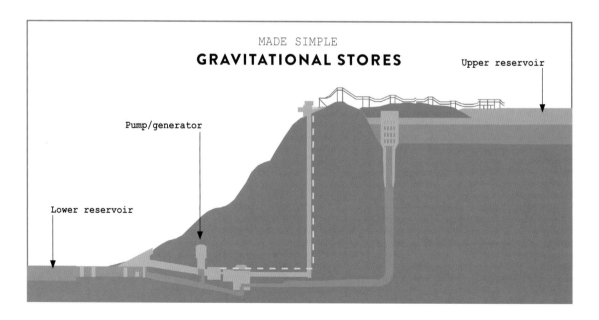

MADE SIMPLE
GRAVITATIONAL STORES

Upper reservoir

Pump/generator

Lower reservoir

Engineers have found ways to make wind turbines more efficient, such as using special materials like carbon fiber to make the blades strong and light. Soon, turbine blades will be up to 328 feet (100 meters) long, the length of a soccer field.

- **Gravitational stores** might involve using unwanted energy to pump water to a high reservoir. When energy is needed, the water is allowed to flow from the reservoir, turning a turbine as it goes.
- **Batteries** can store energy chemically. Another way to do this is to use extra energy to get hydrogen from water. Hydrogen is a clean fuel that only produces water when it burns.
- **A flywheel** is a kinetic store. Extra energy is used to turn a wheel very fast. If it is kept in a vacuum and friction is low, then it will keep turning for a long time. The flywheel can then turn a generator when needed.
- **Molten salt storage** is an example of a thermal store, where unused energy is used to melt salt. The salt can then be used to boil water, as it will stay hot for a number of hours.

FLYWHEEL ENERGY STORAGE DEVICE

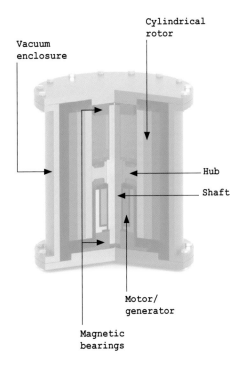

Cylindrical rotor

Vacuum enclosure

Hub

Shaft

Motor/ generator

Magnetic bearings

ANSWER THIS

1. Which gas is mainly responsible for the rise in global temperatures over the last few decades?

2. Other than global warming, what problems can result from burning fuels for energy?

3. How does energy storage help solve the issues associated with wind and solar power?

4. Give an example of a way to store energy kinetically.

POWER AND ENGINEERING

1. **What major innovation 100,000 years ago led humans to be able to survive colder climates?**

   a. Domestication of cattle animals

   b. Bricks for building

   c. Control of fire

   d. Wheels for transportation

2. **Where and when is the earliest known use of waterwheels?**

   a. China in the 15th century

   b. The Middle East in the third or fourth century BC

   c. Ancient Egypt in 2500 BC

   d. England in 1715

3. **Which of these sources does not store energy that originated from the Sun?**

   a. Coal

   b. Biomass

   c. Geothermal

   d. Wind power

4. **What is an electrical current? A flow of:**

   a. Charge

   b. Air

   c. Atoms

   d. Magnets

5. **When did Michael Faraday invent the electric motor?**

   a. 1700

   b. 1800

   c. 1821

   d. 1881

6. **Which of these is not an important part of a chemical cell?**

   a. Anode

   b. Cathode

   c. Electrolyte

   d. Magnet

7. **What is the semiconducting element needed for making solar cells?**

   a. Silicon

   b. Oxygen

   c. Carbon

   d. Uranium

8. **Where was the first public energy supply?**

   a. New York

   b. London

   c. Godalming

   d. San Francisco

9. **What invention allows electricity to travel from power stations through cables with a low current to avoid resistance?**

   a. Generator

   b. Transformer

   c. Resistor

   d. Transistor

10. **How does the level of carbon dioxide in the atmosphere now compare to 250 years ago?**

    a. There is half as much now

    b. There is the same amount

    c. There is one and a half times as much

    d. There is two and a half times as much

Answers on page 214

SIMPLE SUMMARY

Humans get their energy from the food they eat, but we are limited by how much our bodies can store and use at once. Around 100,000 years ago, we learned to control fire to release the energy stored chemically in wood to get more nutrients from our food and to live in colder climates.

- Energy sources are stores of energy, like the wind, that can be made to transfer their energy in a useful way.

- Flowing electricity (or current) and electrostatic forces are caused by the attraction and repulsion due to charge, which is a property of the electrons and protons that make up atoms.

- Charge can flow through a wire in a direct current or in an alternating current.

- Solar cells produce an electric current when hit by light, and piezoelectric materials can even generate electricity from being stretched or squashed.

- Power stations contain generators that need to be turned to generate electricity. Some use the energy released from burning fuels or nuclear reactions to boil water.

- By the 1950s, scientists noticed that our atmosphere was warming, mainly due to an increase in carbon dioxide from the burning of fossil fuels.

- Energy needs have become much greater and there is now two and a half times as much carbon dioxide in the atmosphere as there was 250 years ago.

5
TRANSPORTATION

Wheels, wings, sails, propellers, and engines are innovations that have allowed engineers to make transportation faster, more convenient, safer, and cheaper to use. These changes have changed lives. Only 200 years ago, people rarely went much farther than their own village. Now it is common to travel internationally, and humans have traveled as far as the Moon.

WHAT YOU WILL LEARN

Getting around

Personal transportation

Public transit

Boats and subs

Taking flight

Space and beyond

Future transportation

5.1 GETTING AROUND

Humans are relatively slow and weak. Ancient people often lived near the coast because it was easier to transport heavy objects on boats. The invention of the wheel around 6,000 years ago meant that vehicles could be more easily dragged by mammals like oxen and horses, which are more powerful and cheaper to look after than people. Yet transportation was still slow and expensive. This changed in the 1800s, however, thanks to the invention of the steam engine.

FACT Cars can go much faster than horse-drawn carts, but the average speed of traffic in New York City in 2018 was just 4.7 miles (7.6 km) per hour, which is not much faster than walking speed.

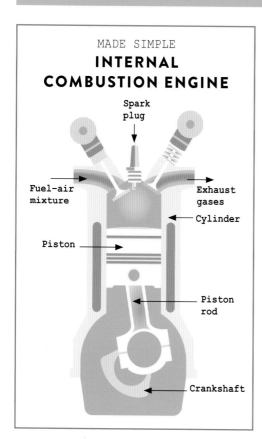

MADE SIMPLE
INTERNAL COMBUSTION ENGINE

Spark plug

Fuel-air mixture

Exhaust gases

Cylinder

Piston

Piston rod

Crankshaft

Steam engines were invented in the early 1700s and were improved greatly by the end of the century, particularly by James Watt, after whom the unit of power is named. In a steam engine, water is boiled by burning a fuel. The steam pushes on a piston that can then be used to turn a wheel. Most vehicles now use internal combustion engines, which were invented in the mid-1800s. A fuel is burned inside the engine and the expanding gases produce push on a piston or a rotor to generate movement. Combustion engines can be smaller than steam engines and are used to power cars, boats, and jets.

When engines burn fuel, pollution is produced. Electric motors produce no emissions and have been around for almost as long as steam engines. They have been used for trams and trains for over 100 years because they can get power through the tracks or overhead cables, but battery technology has prevented them from being popular for cars, until recently.

The open road

Getting around on land is easier when roads are smooth. Before roads, trails were made on busy trade routes by the constant trampling of animals and people. However, they would easily become bumpy, or muddy in the rain, making journeys slow.

The greatest ancient road builders were the Romans, who built over 50,000 miles (80,000 kilometers) of stone roads across Europe. The roads were raised in the middle so that water would drain to the sides, and so required less maintenance, allowing the Romans to send armies more quickly across their vast empire.

ROMAN ROAD CONSTRUCTION

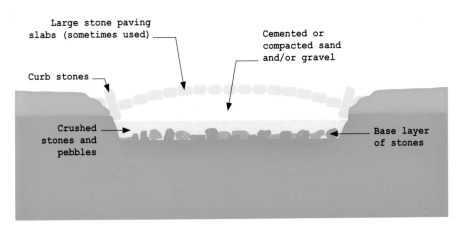

Tar paving was first used in Iraq in the ninth century, but was not widely used elsewhere. However, the invention of the automobile meant that roads needed to be much smoother, so since the early 1900s they have been built with tarmac.

ANSWER THIS

1. How many years ago was the wheel invented?

2. Why has it been easier to have electric transportation on rails than on the road?

3. Why were Roman roads raised in the middle?

4. What substance are modern roads made from?

PERSONAL TRANSPORTATION

Getting around by walking or running is slow and tiring—thankfully, engineers have developed other ways to travel. Jet skis, skateboards, motorcycles, private jets, scooters, caravans, and snowmobiles are all used for personal transportation, but the two most popular alternatives to walking are bicycles and cars—and there are around a billion of each in the world today.

Modern bicycles are incredibly efficient. Cyclists can go four times faster than walkers using the same energy, and the fastest a cyclist has ever gone on a flat surface is close to 183 miles per hour (295 km/h). Amazingly, engineers have achieved this without fully understanding all of the forces that keep bicycles stable, despite them being invented around 150 years ago.

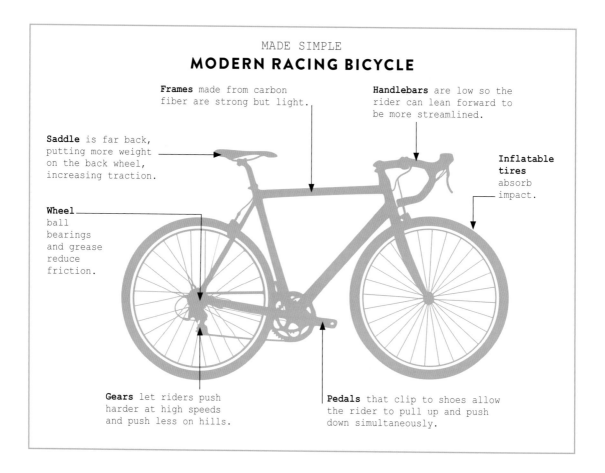

MADE SIMPLE
MODERN RACING BICYCLE

Frames made from carbon fiber are strong but light.

Handlebars are low so the rider can lean forward to be more streamlined.

Saddle is far back, putting more weight on the back wheel, increasing traction.

Inflatable tires absorb impact.

Wheel ball bearings and grease reduce friction.

Gears let riders push harder at high speeds and push less on hills.

Pedals that clip to shoes allow the rider to pull up and push down simultaneously.

Early bicycles were unstable and difficult to steer, as the rider both pedaled and steered with the front wheel. This changed in 1885 when J. K. Starley designed the Rover bicycle with pedals that drove the back wheel with a chain. Soon after, inflatable tires were introduced to absorb impact from bumps, making for a smoother ride. Engineers have found hundreds of other ways to improve bicycle performance, but the basic design has remained the same.

AERODYNAMICS

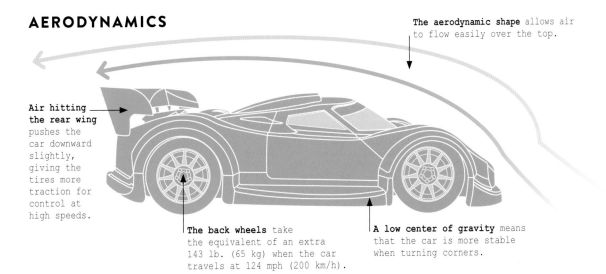

The aerodynamic shape allows air to flow easily over the top.

Air hitting the rear wing pushes the car downward slightly, giving the tires more traction for control at high speeds.

The back wheels take the equivalent of an extra 143 lb. (65 kg) when the car travels at 124 mph (200 km/h).

A low center of gravity means that the car is more stable when turning corners.

Four-wheelers

The convenience and popularity of cars changed the world beyond recognition, allowing cities to expand into suburbs, and goods to become easier and cheaper to transport. However, cars are noisy and dirty and can endanger life. In addition, city layouts have become spread out to accommodate parking and traffic, making less room for outdoor, communal spaces.

For some, cars are simply a way to get around conveniently, but they are also used for sport, fun, or as status symbols. The most expensive car produced for street driving is the Koenigsegg CCXR Trevita. Its body is made from strong but light carbon fiber, and is coated in diamond dust to give it a shimmering silver appearance. Its large engine, streamlined shape, and rear wing help give it a top speed of 254 mph (409 km/h).

ANSWER THIS

1. What are popular forms of personal transportation?

2. What is the purpose of an inflatable tire?

3. Why might you make a bicycle or car from carbon fiber?

4. How do cars attempt to reduce air resistance?

5. What are the disadvantages of cars for transportation?

5.3 PUBLIC TRANSIT

In 1800, an Atlantic crossing took around seven weeks. The journey was dangerous, uncomfortable, and expensive. Today, passenger jets fly the crossing safely in under eight hours. Improvements in public transportation led to big changes in society, allowing businesses, ideas, and people to spread and mix internationally. Public transit lacks the convenience of personal transportation, but is often cheaper and more efficient, as passengers use less road space and share maintenance and fuel costs.

HORSE-DRAWN OMNIBUS

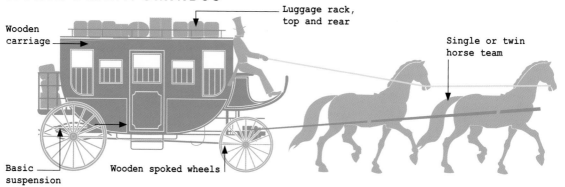

Wooden carriage

Luggage rack, top and rear

Single or twin horse team

Basic suspension

Wooden spoked wheels

In cities, lots of people take lots of short journeys, so transportation needs to stop regularly along set routes. In 1826, Stanislas Baudry was the first person to successfully use this idea in Nantes, France, with his horse-drawn omnibus.

MADE SIMPLE
MAGLEV TRAINS

Maglev (magnetic levitation) trains use two sets of magnets: one set to repel and push the train up off the track, and another set to move the elevated train ahead, taking advantage of the lack of friction.

Baudry thought his omnibus service would encourage people to visit the spa that he ran just outside the town. They did not come to the spa, but the service was so popular that he set up a business in Paris. London had an omnibus within three years.

To avoid transportation taking up much-needed space, many cities have underground railways. The first was the London Underground in 1863, which started with steam trains. The air in the poorly ventilated stations was thick with steam and soot, and people would regularly pass out from the heat and fumes. Electric trains, powered by two electrified rails, were introduced in 1890.

High-speed travel

Cheap air travel lets people travel and work all over the world but also uses a lot of fuel per passenger. It contributes significantly to the carbon dioxide emissions that lead to climate change (see page 86). While trains are slower, they use less fuel, and can still go very fast. The fastest train is the L0 Series maglev train from Japan, which has traveled over 373 mph (600 km/h). It uses electromagnets to float above the track, so has no moving parts to cause friction.

ANSWER THIS

1. What are the advantages of public transit over private transportation?

2. When was the first successful bus service?

3. What was the first underground railway?

4. What is an advantage of trains over airplanes for long-distance travel?

5. Why can maglev trains go faster with less energy?

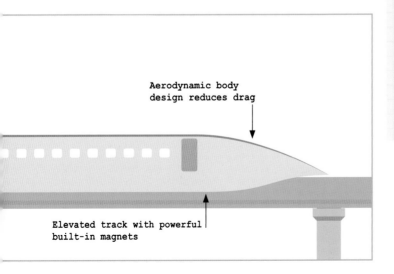

Aerodynamic body design reduces drag

Elevated track with powerful built-in magnets

5.4 BOATS AND SUBS

The first boats were probably made from hollowed-out tree trunks hundreds of thousands of years ago and powered by rowing. As well as being powered by the wind for thousands of years, boats have also been powered by engines and even nuclear reactors. Boats can transport large weights long distances, so are used for sending manufactured goods and oil around the world, but many people sail boats simply for pleasure.

Even though boats have been around much longer, buoyancy was first described by the Greek engineer Archimedes in 212 BC. He realized that the upward force on a floating object equals the weight of fluid pushed out the way. Since 35 cubic feet of water weighs close to 2,200 pounds, a 2,200-pound boat needs a volume bigger than 35 cubic feet, otherwise it will be denser than water and sink.

The Chinese were the first to use a steerable rudder on the back of the boat, in the first century. As the rudder turns, drag increases on one side of the boat and it turns. Keels were a Viking innovation to reduce rocking. Ballast, which is when extra weight is put at the bottom of the boat, also adds stability by lowering the center of gravity.

Powered boats get their thrust from propellers that push water backward as they spin, whereas sailing boats use the wind to push them around. Early sails were square and only worked with the wind behind them. It is not known when triangular sails first appeared, but they allowed for tacking, which is a zigzag motion that lets boats sail into the wind.

Submarines

In 1620, on the river Thames in London, Dutch inventor Cornelis Drebbel demonstrated the first recorded submarine. It was propelled by oars and the journey lasted for over three hours.

Submarines control their depth by pumping water in and out of air tanks to change their buoyancy, but powering a submarine is difficult because fuels need air to burn. Some submarines are powered by batteries for short journeys, or use nuclear reactors to stay underwater for months at a time. Electricity is used to get oxygen from water for breathing, and they need thick metal sides to withstand the enormous pressure deep underwater.

 FACT To freshen the air in his submarine, Drebbel reportedly used a recently discovered chemical reaction that involved heating saltpeter. We now know that the reaction releases oxygen, which is remarkable, because oxygen would not be discovered properly for another 150 years.

MADE SIMPLE
SAILING BOAT

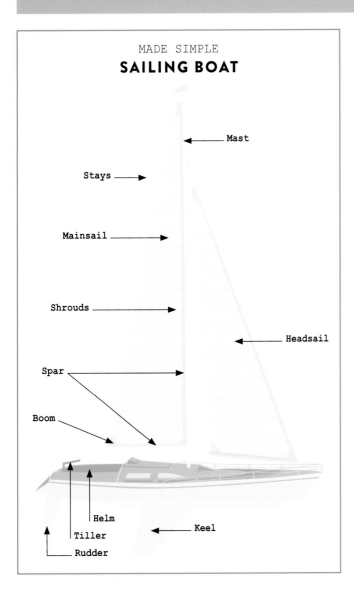

Mast

Stays

Mainsail

Shrouds

Headsail

Spar

Boom

Helm

Tiller

Rudder

Keel

ANSWER THIS

1. List five ways in which a boat can be powered.

2. What is Archimedes' law of buoyancy?

3. How do the forces on a rudder help a boat steer?

4. Why was the triangular sail an important innovation in sailing boat design?

5. How do submarines control their depth?

5.5 TAKING FLIGHT

The first humans to fly used the forces of buoyancy when they boarded a hot-air balloon designed by the Montgolfier brothers in Paris in 1783. Airplanes are lifted by the forces on their wings. By adjusting the shape or angle of the wings, airplanes can move faster than any other form of transportation. The first manned heavier-than-air flight was made by the Wright brothers in North Carolina in 1903.

Aerofoils are shapes designed to get a push on one side more than the other when moving through liquids or gases. There are two ways in which their shape can help an airplane fly. Angling the aerofoil downward means there is more air resistance on the bottom of the wing and it gets pushed upward.

Wings also take advantage of the Bernoulli effect. In 1738, Daniel Bernoulli noticed that faster-moving liquids or gases exert less pressure than slower ones. The air traveling over the top of the wings has farther to go, and so moves faster over the wing than the air under the wing. Since there is less pressure on top than the bottom, the wing is pushed upward.

FACT

The first successful manned helicopter was designed by Slovak inventor Hermann Ganswindt in 1901. It was actually part of a design for a system to launch people into space. The helicopter would take a rocket up and then its dynamite-powered engines would be used to get it into space.

The biggest passenger airliner is the Airbus A380-800. It can carry 850 passengers for 9,200 miles (14,800 km) and its wings can support over 715 tons. It requires four turbofan jets for forward thrust, each 10 feet (3 meters) wide, and all of its controls are electronic. Electronic controls must be tested thoroughly to make sure they cannot fail, but the airplane is fitted with thousands of sensors, making for a safer and smoother flight.

Helicopters and drones

Airplanes need to be moving forward to generate lift on their wings, but helicopters and drones have spinning rotors with tilted aerofoils that allow them to hover. This means that they can take off without a runway, making them useful for flying and landing in crowded or remote areas without runways. They can be used as ambulances to avoid traffic or to get to places that are far from a hospital.

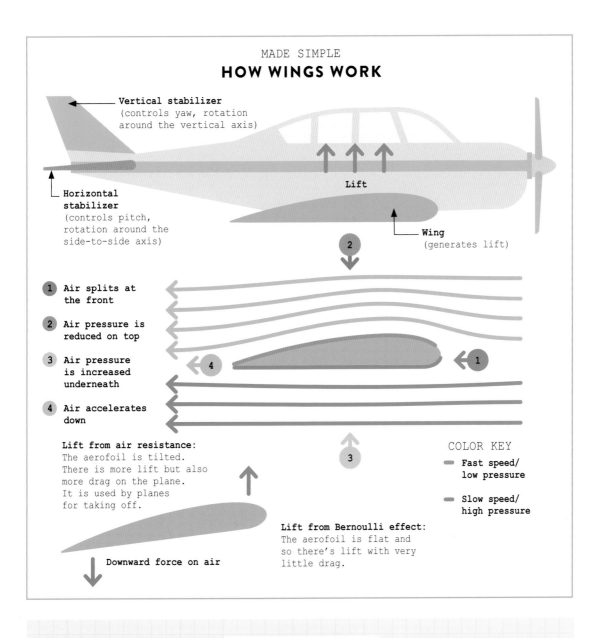

HOW WINGS WORK

Vertical stabilizer
(controls yaw, rotation around the vertical axis)

Lift

Horizontal stabilizer
(controls pitch, rotation around the side-to-side axis)

Wing
(generates lift)

1 Air splits at the front

2 Air pressure is reduced on top

3 Air pressure is increased underneath

4 Air accelerates down

Lift from air resistance:
The aerofoil is tilted. There is more lift but also more drag on the plane. It is used by planes for taking off.

Downward force on air

Lift from Bernoulli effect:
The aerofoil is flat and so there's lift with very little drag.

COLOR KEY
━ Fast speed/ low pressure
━ Slow speed/ high pressure

ANSWER THIS

1. What was the first vehicle to achieve human flight?

2. What is an aerofoil?

3. What are the two ways in which an airplane's wing can generate lift?

4. Why are helicopters sometimes used as ambulances?

LESSON 5.6

SPACE AND BEYOND

To leave the Earth's atmosphere, objects must move at a minimum of 25,020 mph (40,270 km/h). The only way to achieve these speeds is with rockets. Rockets became advanced enough to send people to space after 1945. Until recently, only governments have had the resources to send people into space, but private companies are now developing technology to make space tourism viable in the near future.

During the Cold War, the United States and the Soviet Union competed to outdo each other in the Space Race. In 1957, the Soviets launched the first satellite, *Sputnik*, and then, in 1961, the first human in space, Yuri Gagarin, who completed one orbit of Earth in under two hours.

MADE SIMPLE
APOLLO CREWED LUNAR LANDING

The Apollo Lunar Module was the lander that was flown from lunar orbit to the Moon's surface during the Apollo program. It was the first crewed spacecraft to operate exclusively in the airless vacuum of space, and remains the only crewed vehicle to land anywhere beyond Earth.

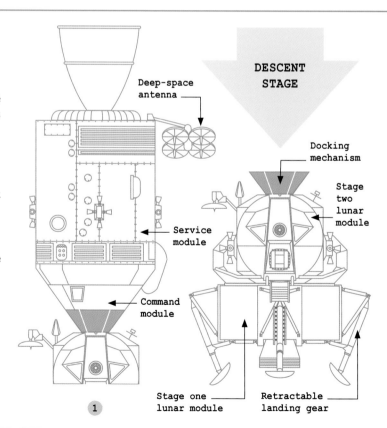

DESCENT STAGE

Deep-space antenna

Docking mechanism

Stage two lunar module

Service module

Command module

Stage one lunar module

Retractable landing gear

1

The Americans responded with the Apollo program to send people to the Moon. It was perhaps the most ambitious engineering project in history, costing over $150 billion and employing over 400,000 people. In 1969, *Apollo 11* was the first of five landings on the Moon, and nobody has been back since 1972.

When the Cold War ended, several countries collaborated to make the International Space Station. It orbits the Earth at a height of 255 miles (410 km) and the astronauts on board do experiments to help us better understand how to prepare for traveling to other planets.

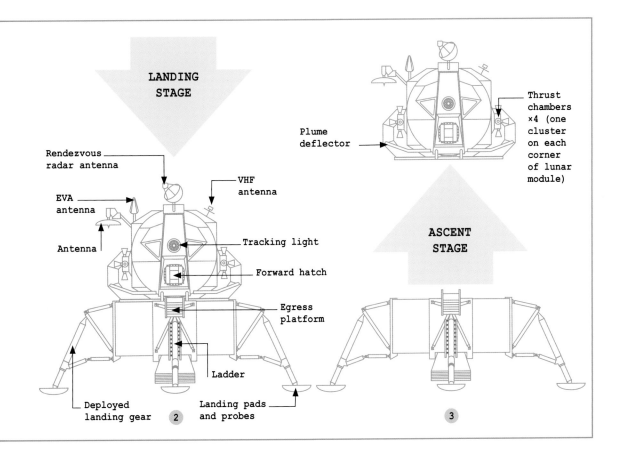

LANDING STAGE

Rendezvous radar antenna

EVA antenna

Antenna

VHF antenna

Tracking light

Forward hatch

Egress platform

Ladder

Deployed landing gear

Landing pads and probes

2

Plume deflector

Thrust chambers ×4 (one cluster on each corner of lunar module)

ASCENT STAGE

3

Why is space travel tricky?

Space travel has a number of challenges, and engineers have developed ingenious solutions to allow humans to leave the Earth's atmosphere:

• **Leaving the atmosphere** Multistage rockets are different rockets joined together which ignite in stages. When the first rockets run out of fuel, they fall off, reducing the weight of the rocket overall. Multistage rockets therefore use less fuel, and can use different rockets and fuels that are optimized for different heights in the atmosphere.

• **Reentry** Spacecraft reentering the atmosphere are traveling over 15,600 mph (25,000 km/h). The air resistance is so great that they heat up dangerously. Engineers discovered that objects heat up less when they are rounded and blunt. They cover the craft in heat-resistant tiles, which keep the inside from getting hot, and a special surface that is designed to absorb heat and then crumble away, taking the heat with it.

• **Living in a vacuum** There is no air in space, so the insides of spacecraft and space suits must have the same air and air pressure as the Earth's surface, to keep astronauts safe. If there is even a tiny hole, air can escape and the pressure will drop fatally. To control the atmosphere inside, spacecraft produce oxygen from water and carry bottled supplies of oxygen as a backup.

• **Floating around** Being in microgravity for extended periods of time causes health problems. Without regular exercise, the heart and other muscles become weaker as they are used less, so spacecraft have exercise machines.

• **Cosmic radiation** Space is full of dangerous radiation that can go through spacecrafts' walls. If humans are exposed to enough, it can kill them. The International Space Station is still protected by the Earth's magnetic field, but interplanetary astronauts might hide in lead chambers when there is a large burst of radiation, or wear special vests that protect the most affected bodily organs.

ASTRONAUT TREADMILL

The Treadmill with Vibration Isolation Stabilization System, or TVIS, is a treadmill for use on board the International Space Station and is designed to allow astronauts to run without vibrating delicate microgravity science experiments in adjacent labs.

FACT

Rockets were originally developed for missile warfare in China in the 13th century.

ANSWER THIS

1. When and where were the first rockets invented?

2. What was the first man-made object in space?

3. List five things that make space travel difficult.

4. How can a spacecraft avoid burning up on reentry into Earth's atmosphere?

5. Why might interplanetary astronauts have to spend time in lead chambers during their long journeys?

5.7 FUTURE TRANSPORTATION

Transportation in the future will enable us to go faster, while being safer. Engineers are always looking for ways to make transportation more convenient, more efficient, and less harmful to our environment. Future transportation will need to be powered without burning fuels that create pollution and contribute to climate change, and computers will take over the controls to increase safety.

FUTURISTIC VEHICLES

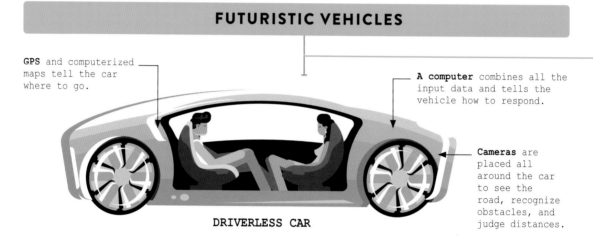

GPS and computerized maps tell the car where to go.

A computer combines all the input data and tells the vehicle how to respond.

Cameras are placed all around the car to see the road, recognize obstacles, and judge distances.

DRIVERLESS CAR

Autonomous driving

An autonomous vehicle is one that can drive itself. As computers and electronic sensors improve, engineers are making them safer than their human-driven counterparts, with quicker reactions than human drivers. A fleet of vehicles that can communicate with one another can drive closer together at greater speeds, as they know when the vehicle in front is about to brake. They can also coordinate their routes and speeds to reduce traffic jams. Autonomous public transit is cheaper to run as there are no drivers, making it more affordable to hire your own and have it drive you wherever you want.

Vactrains

Energy for transportation is used to overcome air resistance, which gets bigger as you go faster, making high-speed travel inefficient. Engineers have suggested maglev trains that travel through tunnels that have had the air removed, allowing them to reach speeds of up to 4,970 mph (8,000 km/h).

1. Why will autonomous vehicles become safer than human-driven ones?

2. How might vacuum tunnels improve long-distance travel?

3. What is the advantage of flying cars?

4. Why will spaceplanes be cheaper to use than multistage rockets?

VACTRAIN

FLYING CAR

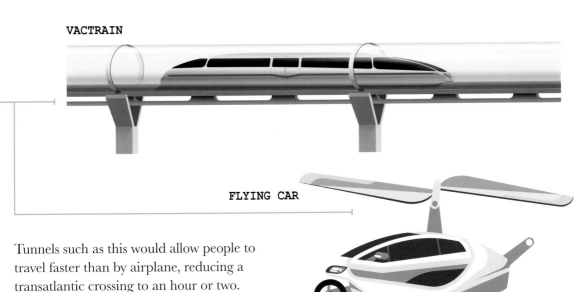

Tunnels such as this would allow people to travel faster than by airplane, reducing a transatlantic crossing to an hour or two.

Future flight

Engineers have already designed flying cars that run on gasoline, such as the PAL-V Liberty, but as battery technology improves, and the demand for space in cities becomes greater, we might see electrically powered cars regularly flying overhead.

Spaceplanes are a combination of a rocket and an airplane. It is much cheaper for them to leave the Earth's atmosphere and land again, as they can behave like an airplane at low altitudes, requiring less fuel overall. Unlike multistage rockets, they do not have engines that drop off, meaning they are reusable—this saves a lot of money. Flying high in the atmosphere means less air resistance, allowing spaceplanes to go faster than normal planes, cutting a transatlantic crossing to just an hour.

TRANSPORTATION

1. **How high above Earth does the International Space Station orbit?**

   a. 1,000 miles (1,600 km)

   b. 1 mile (1.6 km)

   c. 765 miles (1,230 km)

   d. 255 miles (410 km)

2. **What was the earliest mode of transportation?**

   a. Boats

   b. Cars

   c. Trains

   d. Horse and cart

3. **Which of the following was not an advantage of Roman roads?**

   a. They were made with tarmac to be smooth

   b. They were raised in the middle so that water drained away

   c. They were long and straight

   d. They needed very little maintenance

4. **What was J. K. Starley's major innovation that made bicycles more stable?**

   a. The wheels had tires

   b. The back wheels were driven by a chain

   c. The front wheels were driven by a chain

   d. The saddle was farther forward

5. **What material forms the body of the most expensive car ever made?**

   a. Copper

   b. Plastic

   c. Carbon fiber

   d. Steel

6. **What powered the first omnibus in 1826?**

   a. A steam engine

   b. Electric motors

   c. It was pulled by people

   d. It was pulled by horses

7. **What is the purpose of a boat's keel?**

   a. It catches the wind

   b. It steers the boat

   c. It prevents the boat from rocking

   d. It holds the sails up

8. **What was the first machine to fly with humans on board?**

   a. The Wright brothers' airplane

   b. The Montgolfier brothers' hot-air balloon

   c. Ganswindt's helicopter

   d. Drebbel's submarine

9. **What was the purpose of the Apollo space program?**

   a. To send people to the Moon

   b. To send people to the Sun

   c. To send people into orbit

   d. To put a satellite into space

10. **What is an autonomous vehicle?**

    a. A vehicle that has no emissions

    b. A vehicle with automatic gears

    c. A vehicle that can drive and fly

    d. A vehicle that controls itself

Answers on page 215

SIMPLE SUMMARY

Wheels, wings, sails, propellers, and engines are innovations that have allowed engineers to make transportation faster, more convenient, safer, and cheaper to use.

- Steam engines were invented in the early 1700s and were improved greatly by the end of the century, particularly by James Watt, after whom the unit of power is named.

- The greatest ancient road builders were the Romans, who built over 50,000 miles (80,000 kilometers) of stone roads across Europe.

- Cyclists can go four times faster than walkers using the same amount of energy.

- The convenience and popularity of cars changed the world beyond recognition, allowing cities to expand into suburbs, and goods to become easier and cheaper to transport.

- The first underground railway was in London, which started in 1863 with steam trains.

- Powered boats get their thrust from propellers that push water backward as they spin, whereas sailing boats use the wind to push them around.

- Airplanes are lifted by the forces on their wings—the Bernoulli effect.

- In 1969, *Apollo 11* was the first of five landings on the Moon, and nobody has been back since 1972.

- Future transportation will need to be powered without burning fuels that create pollution and contribute to climate change, and computers will take over the controls to increase safety.

6
MACHINES AT WORK

When you think of engineering, one of the first things that comes to mind is the machine. From huge factory units that press out car parts to the humble mousetrap, engineers are responsible for applying the physics of forces to simple materials that make our lives easier.

WHAT YOU WILL LEARN

Simple machines

Machines under power

Measuring time

Robotics

Intelligent machines

Quantum computing

Cool technology

6.1 SIMPLE MACHINES

Of all of the machines you have at home, which is the simplest? Lawn mowers might come to mind, or maybe a clock. They are examples of mechanical devices, and many machines are certainly more complicated. But they are still made of many moving components, such as levers, wheels, pulleys, and screws.

Simple machines are the building blocks of mechanical devices. Here are some examples:

Levers

A broom might not seem like a machine, but it is an object that transforms a short, hard push into a long-distance sweeping motion to move a load. Shovels and even fishing rods are also levers. All levers are beams that change forces by pivoting at a point called the "fulcrum." In this example, one hand forms the fulcrum, while the other applies effort by moving the broom to change the position of a load such as a pile of dust.

Wheels

Wheels are a little like circular levers: by pushing one part a small distance, another part moves a large distance. A shaft called an axle pivots in the center of the wheel, turning in tiny circles. Putting effort into making this part turn will make the larger circle around it turn around as well, covering more ground. Unlike levers, wheels can also turn a horizontal motion into a circular one, changing the direction of a force. This makes it easier to overcome friction—rolling an object is a lot easier than dragging it!

FACT

The word "work" has a specific meaning in physics. It describes the force that makes an object move a certain distance. If you kick a ball into a net 65 feet (20 meters) away, you have done work. Likewise, a machine that lifts a crate 6 feet (2 meters) has also done work. The formula for work is: $W = F \times d$.
F = The force (in newtons) applied in the direction of the object's movement
d = The distance (in feet/meters) an object is moved

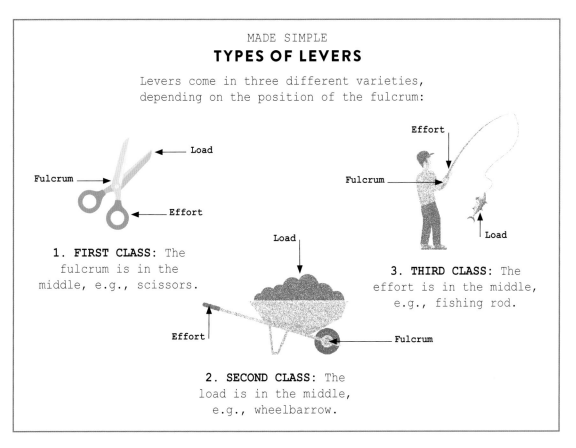

MADE SIMPLE
TYPES OF LEVERS

Levers come in three different varieties,
depending on the position of the fulcrum:

Load

Fulcrum

Effort

1. FIRST CLASS: The
fulcrum is in the
middle, e.g., scissors.

Load

Effort

2. SECOND CLASS: The
load is in the middle,
e.g., wheelbarrow.

Effort

Fulcrum

Load

3. THIRD CLASS: The
effort is in the middle,
e.g., fishing rod.

Fulcrum

Inclined planes

People have marveled at Egypt's ancient pyramids for centuries, wondering how their heavy slabs of sandstone were lifted to such dizzying heights. In reality, little more than a long ramp could have done the trick. A ramp is a surface, or plane, that is tilted. It makes the work of lifting easier by spreading the effort over a long distance.

Consider the act of climbing a steep mountain: it's difficult, even if the distance to the summit is relatively short. Push hard enough, though, and you'll get there in no time. Now imagine a mountain with long sloping sides. As is the case with steps that are more horizontal than vertical, the journey to the top might be easier but it will take longer.

ANSWER THIS

1. What are three examples of a simple machine?

2. What is the pivoting position on a lever called?

3. How do ramps make work easier?

4. What does "work" mean in physics?

LESSON
6.2 MACHINES UNDER POWER

Whether it's a simple pair of scissors or something more complicated like a bicycle, many machines rely on your muscles to cut, dig, lift, spin, or push. But other sources of energy can provide power to do work. These can be just about anything—light from the sun, the chemical bonds in a fossil fuel, or the stored charge in a battery.

Machines that convert energy to produce motion are described as engines. They use simple machines, such as levers and wheels, to convert an energy source into a force that makes a task easier. While engines come in a wide variety of shapes, sizes, materials, and structures, there are only a couple of basic types. One type is based on the expanding volume of a fluid, either after it has been compressed or when it's heated. This heat can come from burning fossil fuels, the radioactivity of atoms, or even the warmth of the sun. Another type of engine comes from the interaction between magnetism and an electrical current. By using flowing electrons to push against a separate magnetic field, a strong enough voltage can force simple machines into motion.

FACT

Units of power are named after James Watt. One watt is the same as one joule of energy being converted per second.

In the early days of steam-powered pumping machines, engineers compared their inventions with work traditionally done by horses, by using units called horsepower. Today, one metric horsepower is the same as 735.5 watts.

Industrial Revolution

Around the middle of the 18th century, the way people made machines began to change. One significant improvement changed how machines were powered. Engines were developed that could convert expanding steam into large amounts of work. While steam engines had been around for centuries, better crafting techniques and improved designs in the 17th and 18th centuries meant engines could produce much more power and be easier to control. This meant larger machines that could weave, dig, pump, and transport with unprecedented speed and strength.

The first practical steam engines were made to remove water from flooded mines. An English engineer named Thomas Savery applied the physics of pressure cooking to develop an engine based on a piston moving up and down inside a cylinder. Improvements to Savery's model led to a system of pipes and chambers that could cool and heat water without losing it as steam.

By the late 1700s, Scottish inventor James Watt had added features to steam-driven engines that made them easier to control and more efficient, sparking the Industrial Revolution.

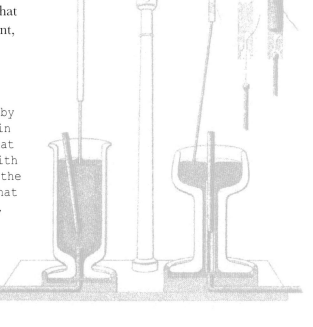

THE FIRST ELECTRIC MOTOR (RIGHT)

The first electric engine was made by English scientist Michael Faraday in 1821. He hung a wire in a vessel that contained a magnet and was filled with mercury. When a current ran through the wire, it created a magnetic field that pushed against the magnet's field, causing the wire to rotate.

AEOLIPILE (LEFT)

One of the earliest records of a steam-powered engine dates back 2,000 years. An engineer named Hero of Alexandria came up with a device called an aeolipile. When water inside its chamber was heated, the resulting steam would shoot from a pair of tubes, causing the device to spin on an axis.

ANSWER THIS

1. What do engines do?

2. What are two basic types of engines?

3. What is horsepower a measure of?

4. How did engines change in the 18th century?

5. What were the first steam engines designed to do?

MEASURING TIME

In today's busy world, every second counts. Thanks to centuries—if not millennia—of innovation in engineering, we can also count every second.

Ancient sundials and hourglasses have long managed to do a reasonable job of keeping track of time passing. By the 14th century, a toothed ring called an escapement was making it possible to invent devices that could accurately divide up the day into precise fractions. It's not entirely clear who first came up with the mechanical component, or how it came to be used in the first medieval timekeeping devices, but this simple item made it possible to create machines that could convert energy into a consistent force capable of measuring out precise units of time. These were the first clocks.

In 1656, a Dutch scientist named Christiaan Huygens used discoveries on the pendulum's swing to come up with the first pendulum clock. A swinging weight kept a precise time, and the teeth on the slowly turning escapement kept nudging the pendulum in constant motion. Falling weights or a spring could then keep the escapement turning, producing an incredibly accurate timekeeping machine.

A machine before its time
In 1900, sponge divers near the Mediterranean island of Antikythera stumbled upon the ancient remains of a sunken ship. Among the many artifacts inside were clumps of rock with strange, gearlike shapes jutting from its surface. For more than a century, historians and engineers have studied these heavily encrusted blocks, using X-ray scans to get a better look at the hidden components. While some suspected it could be pieces of some sort of astronomical clock, others felt it was too complex for something so ancient.

Today, most scholars agree that the roughly 2,000-year-old Antikythera mechanism is one of the oldest known examples of an analog computer. It was most likely used to accurately calculate the positions of the Sun and Moon, dates of eclipses, and maybe even positions of planets.

1. What device made it possible to turn a power source into a consistent stream of energy to measure time?

2. Who invented the first pendulum clock in 1656?

3. What does the combining of gears of different sizes achieve?

4. What was found off the Mediterranean island of Antikythera in 1900?

5. What might the Antikythera mechanism have once been used for?

MADE SIMPLE
HOW GEARS WORK

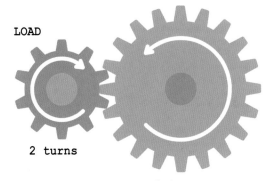

LOAD

**DRIVER
(effort)**

2 turns

1 turn
low force

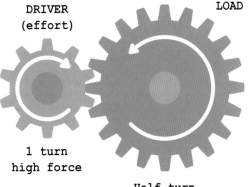

**DRIVER
(effort)**

LOAD

1 turn
high force

Half turn

The radius of a gear acts a little like a lever pivoting on the axle. Small gears have more force, but each rotation covers only a small distance. Big gears cover more distance, with less force.

Locking a small gear with a big gear means that for every rotation of the larger gear, the smaller one has to spin faster to keep up.

Combining gears allows engineers to exchange speed for force (or vice versa), or change the direction of a rotation in a machine.

6.4 ROBOTICS

Quick challenge: Name a famous robot. Maybe C-3PO or R2-D2 from *Star Wars* come to mind. Or a Transformer, like Optimus Prime. In spite of decades of telling stories about machines that think like humans, nobody knows exactly what makes a machine a robot.

Most engineers would agree that one thing all robots have in common is an ability to carry out tasks without needing a human to direct them. That means they don't need arms and legs, or even an ability to communicate in beeps and boops. As long as it has some way of being able to respond to changes in the environment on its own in a useful way, a machine can be considered to be robotic.

Robotic systems have been around for quite some time, carrying out repetitive and dangerous tasks that humans would rather not do. These include mechanical arms that put car parts together, and rolling about over the floor sucking up dust and crumbs. One day, the computers controlling robots might be smart enough to command a steady hand to carry out delicate surgery.

FACT

The word "robot" first appeared in a 1920 play written by a Czech novelist named Karel Čapek, called *Rossum's Universal Robots*. They weren't mechanical helpers, but instead were described as human slaves made from a strange lifelike gel.

Real-life Martians

Up on the surface of Mars, a robot called Opportunity lies in a dusty grave. The machine was active for 15 years, much longer than the three months NASA's engineers had planned for. However, in early 2019, after a lengthy dust storm blocked the sunlight the robot needed to charge its batteries, Opportunity finally stopped working.

Like other mobile machines called rovers that had been sent up to explore the planet, Opportunity had a number of instruments it could use to study the rocks and landscape. Importantly, it could also work out its position using the Sun's position and determine the best path to take to its next destination.

VAUCANSON'S AUTOMATIC DUCK

Bill

Pump

Clockwork

Intestinal tub

Mill for grinding grain

While computers paved the way to truly automated machines, people have been looking for ways to replicate life in machine form for centuries.
In 1739, French inventor Jacques de Vaucanson revealed his amazing masterpiece: a duck that ate food and, well, pooped. Sadly, the famous machine didn't really digest food. Like many inventors, Vaucanson cheated. He used pre-made poop pellets.

ANSWER THIS

1. What makes a machine a robot?

2. What is an example of an actual task performed by a robot?

3. What is the name of the robot rover on Mars that stopped operating in 2019?

4. How long does it take for a radio signal from Earth to reach Mars?

5. Where does the word "robot" come from?

Depending on distance, it can take anywhere from 4 to 24 minutes for radio signals to move from Earth to Mars. It can be a long, slow conversation to give a machine the information it needs to operate. Having a robot make some decisions on its own helps. Future rovers will be even more robotic, choosing which rocks to study and even where to move next all on their own.

LESSON 6.5

INTELLIGENT MACHINES

There are some things computers and brains do that are similar. Both are systems that take in information and process it in a variety of ways to solve problems, for example; but the way in which they do this is rather different.

An early name for the kinds of computers we use today is a "universal Turing machine." They were named after Alan Turing, a 20th-century British mathematician who imagined a single machine that was capable of processing any set of instructions called algorithms. While earlier calculation machines were designed with a specific algorithm in mind, Turing's work inspired machines that used logical rules to work like any calculating device, turning information into a solution to just about any problem.

COLLECTOR

BASE

EMITTER

MADE SIMPLE
TRANSISTOR

Transistors are devices that boost currents, and act like an on/off switch. They are connected to three paths—one for current to enter (emitter), one for it to leave (collector), and a "traffic signal" in the middle (base).

The emitter and collector are made of materials that can build up negative charges. The base is made of a material that has "gaps" of negative charge that usually block currents, keeping it switched off.

A small charge sent into the base fills those gaps, allowing a big current to flow from the emitter to the collector. This boosts signals, and turns the transistor's switch to "on." A whole lot of on/off switches can be used to represent a code for carrying out calculations.

On the other hand, computers use different components to do calculations and retain memory. While different areas of your brain focus on unique tasks, each neuron is like a tiny processor that both remembers and calculates. Computer engineers are working on ways to make technology that can also do this. Called neuromorphic computing, it should lead to even faster ways to process algorithms.

What is AI?

Making a computer that can do all of the things a human brain can do would be awesome—engineers have been working on that for some time. One thing we do well is change our mind when surprising information appears, and then remember it for next time. This ability to solve complex problems and adapt to new information is how we define intelligence. When computers do it, we call it artificial intelligence, or AI.

Intelligent software is increasingly becoming a big deal in technology. It is often made of special lists of algorithms that can carry out a task and then alter its instructions depending on the solution to a problem. AI programs are being developed by software engineers that can find patterns in all kinds of data, and then use it in new and creative ways, from painting masterpieces to designing new medicines.

ANSWER THIS

1. How did Turing's universal computer differ from other calculating machines?

2. What is neuromorphic computing?

3. What do the letters "AI" stand for in computing?

4. What are the two problems behind making a conscious computer?

5. What is the switch-like component that makes today's computers work?

QUANTUM COMPUTING

More than a century ago, scientists thought they had physics mostly figured out. That quickly changed, with experiments on light and subatomic particles showing that the universe is far stranger than we could ever imagine on a tiny, tiny scale.

The word "quantum" simply means "a portion." It came to refer to the discovery that light waves can behave as if they are divided into particle-like pieces, or quanta. Stranger still, it was later found that the particles making up seemingly solid matter also act a little like waves of . . . well, something. Quantum physics is full of strange concepts we find hard to picture—but that hasn't stopped engineers from using these principles to come up with new kinds of electronics. Quantum technology is being used in new ways to measure and image materials, encrypt messages, and even carry out complex calculations.

Bits and qubits

In classical physics, a ball rolling along a table has a clear position and speed. You know exactly where it is and where it is going. In quantum physics, these properties aren't calculated as certainties. They're calculated as a probability. This isn't all that important for big things like soccer balls and cats, but for particles like electrons and photons, these measurements of probability are essential. Your desktop computer performs calculations using the positions of switches to encode certain mathematical functions. Like a light switch, this is on or off. In computing, we say this is binary, represented by a 1 or a 0. This single unit of information is called a bit.

Quantum computing is completely different. The functions are encoded in the way a particle's on or off state is determined by probabilities. While a property—such as a type of momentum called spin—can be in one of two states, when it isn't measured it still exists in a "yet to be determined" position called a superposition. Stranger still, these measurements can depend on similar positions of other particles. Two or more particles can be linked (entangled), which also determines its states. This means a single particle can have three states instead of two. It's not a normal bit—it's a quantum bit. A qubit.

The fuzzy physics behind qubits can be used to solve algorithms that would take a huge number of bits to represent. Quantum computers might never replace your desktop, but they will one day be used to solve problems even the fastest supercomputer would take far too long to crack.

ANSWER THIS

1. What does the word "quantum" mean in quantum physics?

2. Particles in classical physics have a clearly defined position. How is the position of particles described in quantum physics?

3. What is a single unit of information in computing called?

4. What is a superposition?

5. What are quantum computers hoped to achieve one day?

SCHRÖDINGER'S CAT

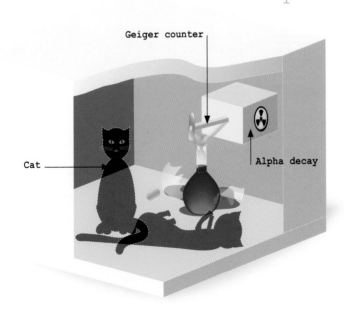

Geiger counter

Cat

Alpha decay

In the 1930s, physicist Erwin Schrödinger disagreed that particles could be in different states before they were measured. He described a scenario where radioactive atoms both broke down and stayed intact at once. A counter would smash a vial of poison when it detected this breakdown, killing a cat in a closed box. Only on looking inside the box would a person know if the cat had died and the atom had broken down. If the atom had decayed and stayed intact, the cat would be both dead and alive, an absurd thing to Schrödinger.

COOL TECHNOLOGY

It's easy to take ice for granted. No matter where you are in the world, you'll probably have easy access to tiny cubes of frozen water. Not only is it great in a cool drink on a warm day, but creating the low temperatures needed for ice today plays an important role in keeping food from spoiling.

Before refrigeration technology was invented, ice from mountaintops or left over from the winter could be packed in straw and stored in specially designed structures called ice houses. One of the earliest mentions of these buildings dates back to around 1780 BC in Mesopotamia, so they've been around for some time.

Some of these buildings were partially or completely below the ground, taking advantage of the insulating properties of the rock and soil. Most also had thick walls, with a door that pointed north to keep out sunlight. While the ice did melt, it usually remained just long enough until it could be refilled with a fresh supply.

The first refrigerators

Take a liquid that can evaporate easily, such as diethyl ether, and place it in a container. Pump out most of the air, and its particles will have so much free space to move about they'll fly around as a gas. Doing this takes a bit of heat energy, though, which the particles steal from the environment, making it cold.

This was the principle Scottish physician William Cullen wanted to show a university audience in the late 18th century. He had no plans to make use of the idea for anything practical, but just under a century later, the first

 FACT Chlorofluorocarbons (CFCs) became inexpensive to manufacture in the 1950s, so became a popular chemical in vapor-based cooling. It was soon discovered that the molecules were destroying ozone in the atmosphere. As we rely on a layer of ozone to help screen out radiation, CFCs were slowly phased out in favor of other cooling chemicals.

refrigeration device was constructed in America by inventor Jacob Perkins. It relied on a similar process as Cullen's idea—a fluid changes phase, taking energy from its environment. The resulting gas is then pumped into an area where heat is removed again, turning it back into a liquid, in a cycle that can keep going around.

Most refrigerators are still run this way, but it is changing. Future technology using crystals that absorb energy as they change shape could be more energy-efficient, and safer for the environment.

HOW DOES A MODERN FRIDGE WORK?

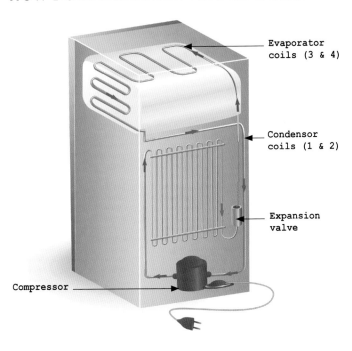

Evaporator coils (3 & 4)

Condensor coils (1 & 2)

Expansion valve

Compressor

1. Warm vapor enters the condensing coils under high pressure, where it releases heat and turns to liquid.
2. Cool liquid leaves the condensing coils under high pressure.
3. Cool liquid enters the evaporating coils under low pressure, where it absorbs heat and turns to vapor.
4. Warm vapor leaves the evaporating coils under low pressure.

ANSWER THIS

1. How was food kept cold before the invention of refrigerators?

2. What process did William Cullen present to a university audience in the 18th century?

3. Who engineered the first refrigeration device?

4. How might refrigerators work in the future?

MACHINES AT WORK

1. **What sort of simple machine is a broom?**

   a. A pulley

   b. A lever

   c. A ramp

   d. A broom is not a machine

2. **What is the formula to calculate "work" in physics?**

   a. Work = friction × direction

   b. Work = force × displacement

   c. Work = friction × distance

   d. Work = fulcrum × load

3. **Which of the following is a source of heat for powering machines?**

   a. Burning fossil fuels

   b. Radiation from decaying atoms

   c. Light from the sun

   d. All of the above

4. **What inspired the English engineer Thomas Savery to devise one of the first engines?**

   a. Egg timers

   b. Frying pans

   c. Pressure cookers

   d. Coffee plungers

5. **What is an escapement?**

   a. A weight that swings back and forth once per second

   b. A toothed ring that helps divide a source of energy into precise units

   c. The face of a clock, divided into 12 sections

   d. A spring that allowed clocks to be worn on the wrist

6. **What kind of clock did the Dutch scientist Christiaan Huygens come up with in the 17th century?**

   a. Water clock

   b. Sundial

   c. Pendulum clock

   d. Digital clock

7. **What feature makes C-3PO in *Star Wars* a true robot?**

   a. He is made of metal

   b. He looks like a human

   c. He must obey humans

   d. He can carry out certain tasks without direct instruction

8. **Why did the Mars rover Opportunity stop working in 2019?**

   a. A dust storm blocked the sunlight the robot needed to charge its batteries

   b. It ran out of methane

   c. NASA switched it off, because its mission was over

   d. It fell down a hole

Answers on page 216

SIMPLE SUMMARY

From huge factory units that press out car parts to the humble mousetrap, engineers are responsible for applying the physics of forces to simple materials that make our lives easier.

• Simple machines, such as levers, wheels, and inclined planes, are the building blocks of mechanical devices.

• Machines that convert energy to produce motion are described as engines. They use simple machines to convert an energy source into a force that makes a task easier.

• In 1656, a Dutch scientist named Christiaan Huygens used discoveries on the pendulum's swing to come up with the first pendulum clock.

• Most engineers would agree that one thing all robots have in common is an ability to carry out tasks without needing a human to direct them.

• Alan Turing was a 20th-century British mathematician who imagined a single machine that was capable of processing any set of instructions called algorithms.

• The word "quantum" simply means "a portion." It came to refer to the discovery that light waves can behave as if they are divided into particle-like pieces, or quanta.

• Refrigeration involves taking a liquid that can evaporate easily, such as diethyl ether, in a container and pumping out most of the air, so its particles fly around as a gas. The heat energy required for this is taken by the particles from the environment, making it cold.

7
CHEMICAL ENGINEERING

Engineering isn't just a matter of building big things—it's often about the building blocks themselves. Chemical engineering involves the application of physics, biology, and chemistry to develop new and better materials that are more suited for a specific task.

WHAT YOU WILL LEARN

Alchemy—magic or engineering?

Smelting through the ages

Reflection and darkness

Problems with plastics

Fertile grounds

Engineering and sports

LESSON 7.1

ALCHEMY—MAGIC OR ENGINEERING?

For thousands of years, people have been trying to solve a seemingly simple question: Why do materials change? Why does wood turn black when it burns? Why does solid ice turn to liquid water when it melts? Why do dull rocks turn to shiny metal when heated?

The oldest examples of discussions on the question "What is everything made out of?" took place in ancient Greece around 2,500 years ago. Philosophers like Democritus of Abdera were the first to suggest all matter was made of small, indivisible units which he called "atoma." Some of these ancient thinkers, such as Aristotle, thought there were four types of basic materials that combined into all things. These were fire, water, air, and earth.

MADE SIMPLE
ALCHEMY SYMBOLS

Alchemists, like today's chemists, simplified names for materials to make it easier to record their observations. It also helped keep their work a secret.

THREE PRINCIPLES   **THE FOUR ELEMENTS**

Mercury   Salt   Sulfur   Air   Earth   Fire   Water

Over time, models explaining what everything is made out of have slowly improved, from models like tiny billiard balls, to little puddings, to solar systems, to strange clouds of possibility.

  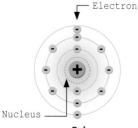

Dalton billiard ball model

Thomson plum pudding model

Rutherford model

Electron

Nucleus

Bohr model

Over the centuries, practices from ancient Egypt had combined with Greek philosophy on matter to form a system called "alchemy" (a word mostly likely from Arabic, meaning "from Egypt"). These practices involved mixing solutions in order to turn "imperfect" mixes of elements into perfect ones—the most perfect of all being gold. One goal was to find a way to make living material so perfect it wouldn't sicken or die.

The road to chemistry

Alchemists often worked in secret, studying how materials broke down and recombined. Their methods of distillation, evaporation, precipitation, and filtering informed future studies we refer to as chemistry. In many ways, alchemists were the first chemical engineers. They applied their discoveries to purify metals, create new kinds of pigment, and improve ceramics. Unfortunately, many of their explanations were supernatural and spiritual rather than based on pure experimentation, making it more trial and error than scientific.

By the 17th century, natural philosophers were coming up with simpler laws to describe what they observed. In 1661 the English scholar Robert Boyle questioned the existence of Aristotle's four fundamental elements in his writings, *The Sceptical Chymist*. His ideas were the start of a new way of thinking about elements which would eventually set the foundations of modern chemistry.

ANSWER THIS

1. When did philosophers first start thinking about the basic nature of matter?

2. What did Democritus of Abdera think everything was made out of?

3. What were the four basic elements of matter according to Aristotle?

4. Who wrote a text in 1661 questioning Aristotle's explanations of matter?

LESSON 7.2

SMELTING THROUGH THE AGES

With few exceptions, just about every shiny, malleable piece of metal in the world was once inside a dull, brittle rock. The chemistry of metals means that highly useful elements such as copper and lead react easily with other elements to form less useful compounds. Just think about how easily iron can combine with oxygen to form rust, or iron oxide.

In nature, mixes of potentially useful metal or other minerals in the form of compounds are called ores. Separating out the mineral from the mess takes some ingenuity, including a few tricks our ancestors discovered thousands of years ago.

TIMELINE OF METALLURGY

Awl discovery: The corroded remains of a small copper spike were dug up at an archaeological site in Israel in 2007. The site was a flourishing town from 5200 to 4600 BC, so the awl could be the oldest evidence of a metal artifact, most likely made from naturally occurring mixes of copper and tin.

Copper Age: This prehistoric period in the Middle East and Mesopotamia lasted from around 5000 BC to 4000 BC. People made copper items without combining it with tin.

| 5200 BC | | 5000 BC | THE COPPER AGE |

Smelting: Roughly 7,000 years ago, copper was being produced from ore by smelting, in today's Serbia. Archaeologists base this claim on their dating of a clump of waste minerals called slag, which was excavated from a site containing evidence of an ancient Neolithic culture called the Vinča.

Copper cooks

There's little doubt that one of the biggest advances in engineering occurred more than 7,000 years ago when people living near the Mediterranean intentionally extracted copper from the green ore malachite in significant quantities for the first time. The hard, lustrous metal could be molded or beaten into jewelry or weapons that impacted on trade and warfare. The practice of using heat and carbon to separate a metal such as copper out from the mix of elements making up its ore is called smelting. It likely developed with kiln technology that heated pottery.

First, the heat "roasts" the ore, breaking down a chemical called copper carbonate hydroxide into water, carbon dioxide, and copper oxide. This occurs at fairly low temperatures of around 500°F (250°C). To remove the oxygen from the copper, temperatures of well more than 1,800°F (1,000°C) are needed. Carbon in the burned wood releases the gas carbon monoxide as it's heated. As this molecule moves past the heated copper oxide, it pulls away oxygen, leaving both pure copper and waste materials called "slag."

Piles of slag: Left over from a bloomery in the Jordanian site of Tell Hammeh, these are considered to be the oldest evidence of iron smelting, dated to around 900 BC. Improved smelting in the first millennium BC in the Middle East brought more iron artifacts, marking the start of the Iron Age.

Copper and tinfoil: A piece of foil uncovered from Pločnik in Serbia could be the earliest example of a bronze artifact. By 3300 BC, objects made from the alloy were being created in cultures across the Middle East, marking the start of the first Bronze Age.

4500 BC   3000 BC   1200 BC

Iron artifacts: Iron smelting has only been around for several thousand years, but iron artifacts date back to around 3000 BC. Iron beads found in a tomb in Gerzeh, Egypt, are among the oldest examples. They seem to have been made from the pure iron found inside meteorites.

Ironing out the details

While easy to extract, copper is a rather soft metal. Early chemical engineers managed to turn copper into a harder material by combining it with tin. The alloy, called bronze, became widespread across the ancient world, and was used in everything from cooking to warfare.

Extracting harder metals like iron from ore required significant changes in methods and technology that could create the right temperatures under the right conditions. It's not clear how these methods were developed, with some scholars thinking small amounts of iron were accidentally produced while smelting copper in some regions. Early iron production was done in a furnace called a "bloomery." Temperatures in this furnace are hot enough for smelting, but not hot enough to melt the iron into a liquid. The resulting metal is a spongy material called "bloom," which ancient blacksmiths could heat and hammer into simple tools that were harder and more durable than bronze.

FACT

Know your iron. Pig iron is a crude mix of iron and significant amounts of carbon (roughly 3 percent) and other impurities, which makes it brittle. Cast iron is more pure, with roughly the same carbon (2 to 4 percent) and, though brittle, has a low melting point that makes it easier to cast. Wrought iron has less than 0.08 percent carbon, and is extremely tough and durable.

BLAST FURNACE

Air is forced in to heat the starting materials of coke (burned fossil fuel with high amounts of carbon), limestone (purifying agent made from calcium carbonate), and an ore. Impurities called slag float on the molten metal.

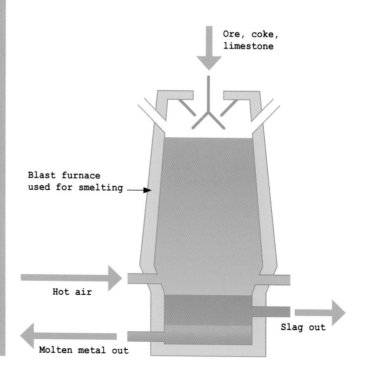

Ore, coke, limestone

Blast furnace used for smelting →

Hot air

Slag out

Molten metal out

Extracting metals with electricity

Aluminum ore is a material called bauxite. Smelting can't be used to separate the metal; it needs to be split with electricity in a process called electrolysis.

- Aluminum oxide is dissolved in a substance called molten cryolite.
- The resulting oxide ions give up electrodes at the positive electrode (anode) to form bubbles of oxygen.
- Positive aluminum ions pick up electrons from the negative electrode (cathode) to become metallic aluminum, which is removed.

ANSWER THIS

1. What is an ore?

2. What is the process of separating useful metals or minerals from their ore using heat and carbon?

3. What is one kind of metal that isn't found in an ore?

4. What kinds of furnaces were used to smelt iron more than 3,000 years ago in the ancient site of Tell Hammeh?

5. How is aluminum separated from its ore?

ELECTROLYSIS

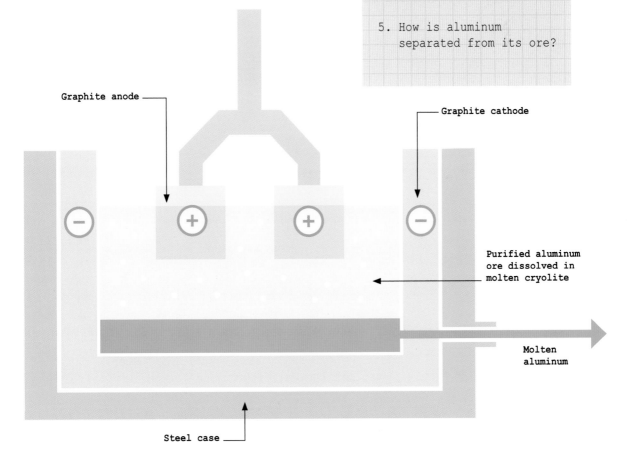

Graphite anode

Graphite cathode

Purified aluminum ore dissolved in molten cryolite

Molten aluminum

Steel case

REFLECTION AND DARKNESS

Nature is full of stunning colors. Sadly, most of them are fleeting. While humans have been making art for tens of thousands of years, the colors they had to choose from were often limited to the black of charcoal or the reds and yellows of ocher.

Colored chemicals called pigments emit color by soaking up, or absorbing, wavelengths from the mix of radiation in white light. What they don't absorb bounces back out, which we see as color. Many of these natural pigments have been used throughout history. Textiles have been dyed blue using dyes made from plants like woad and indigo, for example, while crushed cochineal bugs have been used to create red pigments for cloth, paint, and even food.

To engineer novel pigments that can color anything from pants to paper, tattoos to tapestries, and icing to eyeliner, chemists throughout history have looked for ways to combine minerals into a variety of hues and shades that are durable and nontoxic. Today's global industry for making pigments could be worth as much as $30 billion, with engineers producing bright new colors for all kinds of applications.

MADE SIMPLE
BUILDING BLUES

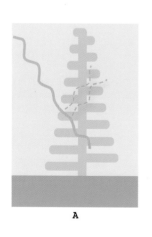

Unlike many other colors, most of the blue we see in the living world is produced by blue light being scattered into our eyes, rather than absorbed and emitted. In picture A, red waves hitting microscopic ridges on a butterfly's wing are absorbed. Blue waves in picture B, on the other hand, are easily scattered out again by the ridges.

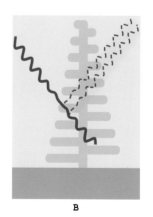

A

B

BLOWN AWAY BY LIGHT

To cover the vast distances of space that exist between the Sun and the closest stars, it might be possible to engineer a special sail that reflects sunlight. These "solar sails" would need to be large and extremely light to be pushed by the small force of a speedy photon of light.

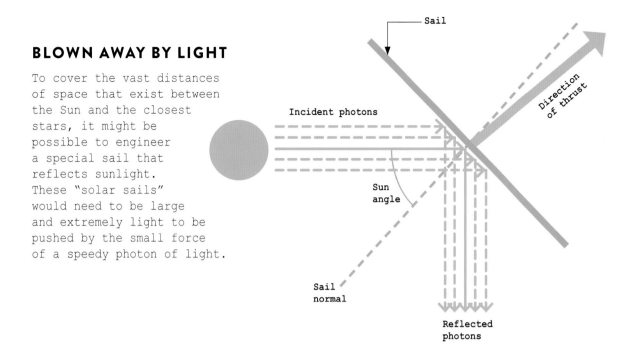

Radiant reflections

While some engineers are interested in creating materials that can absorb light in special ways, others are focused on finding better ways to accurately reflect or bend light.

Your bathroom mirror works thanks to the way light waves interact with the atoms in the glass and the metallic substance coating its rear side. If it's smooth enough, rays of incoming (or "incident") light waves will mostly bounce off (or "reflect") at similar angles, preserving an image you see as a reflection. A lot of the light that hits your bathroom mirror is absorbed or scattered rather than reflected with precision. It's good enough for doing your makeup or brushing your teeth, but many tools in science need near-perfect reflections.

To bounce and bend light in creative ways, engineers can make use of metamaterials. These are artificial substances that have properties that come from their unique structure rather than just its mix of ingredients. Many have fine structures that can reflect, refract, or absorb light in ways that no natural material can manage. Some metamaterials have the potential to guide incoming light around an object. Though it might not hide any young wizards, an "invisibility cloak" made from such a material could warp microwaves or radio waves to improve satellite antennae, or one day make ships and aircraft disappear from radar.

PROBLEMS WITH PLASTICS

It's hard to believe that the first examples of plastic were developed not even two centuries ago. Since then, we've invented many different types to suit many different uses.

All plastics are strings—or polymers—of carbon-based molecules all tangled up. Adding other chemicals to the mix can keep the web of polymers flexible, or harden it into just about any shape. The source of the carbon molecules many plastics are based on is crude oil, which makes the material cheap and easy to make.

These factors have helped plastics not only fill just about every need, but become easily disposable, commonly as a single-use item. Since they aren't easily broken down in the environment, plastic waste has built up. Today, no part of the globe is untouched by the material, with broken-down fragments called microplastics even being found in the deepest parts of the oceans.

The plastic cycle

One thing we can all do to minimize plastic waste is to reduce, reuse, and recycle. In general, there are two ways to do this—mechanically and chemically.

- **Mechanical recycling** involves turning the used plastic into a granule or powder for melting into a new product such as plastic furniture. The used plastic item is washed and cut down into small pieces before being melted down. The polymers break down when this happens, so products made from mechanically recycled plastic pellets can't be recycled themselves. Most plastic is recycled this way.

- **Chemical recycling** involves turning the carbon polymers back into single "links" called monomers. Polyethylene terephthalate (PET) is a common plastic used to make transparent containers. Mixed with ethylene glycol, it breaks down into much shorter chains, which can be melted easily before being turned into simpler units.

Not all plastic items are recyclable this way. To make polymers softer, harder, or more colorful, additives are often mixed in to change the properties of the material. These additives can't be easily removed, and would risk contaminating the process. A new kind of polymer called polydiketoenamine (PDK) might solve that problem. Chemical engineers designed the chains with bonds that break down easily in acid, finding it can be separated from additives far more easily.

Solutions such as this can help, but engineers need to devise new ways to not just clean up plastics, but to make it easily affordable. Some are exploring ways of turning the carbon in plastic polymers back into a hydrocarbon, like the material making up oil. This diesel-like product would be valuable as a source for fuel. It's not a perfect solution to plastic waste, but with so much trash piling up, finding an economical way to transform trash into treasure could be just what we need.

INCREASE IN PLASTIC PRODUCTION

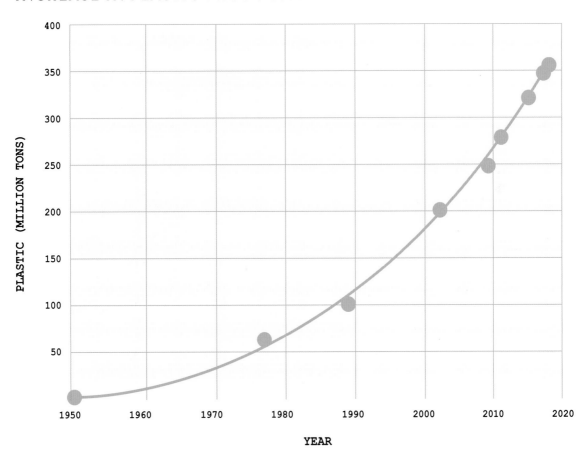

Future of plastics

For as long as we need cheap, easily produced goods, plastics will continue to play an important role in our lives. But it doesn't need to be all bad news. The growing field of bioplastics could one day replace many of the unsustainable polymers we currently depend on.

Bioplastics are a family of materials based on carbon polymers that aren't made from oil, or can easily break down in the environment. While some might still be made from fossil fuels, others could be created from a variety of living sources, such as the shells of crustaceans and insects, or plants and even bacteria grown in a tank.

GREAT PACIFIC GARBAGE PATCHES

Across the Pacific Ocean, there are vast currents that move in circles, called "gyres." They act like huge whirlpools, trapping floating material in the center. Two of these form what's called the Great Pacific Garbage Patch. They are regions where bits of plastic—from microscopic fragments to whole objects—pile up. Most of this waste is from marine industries, like fishing.

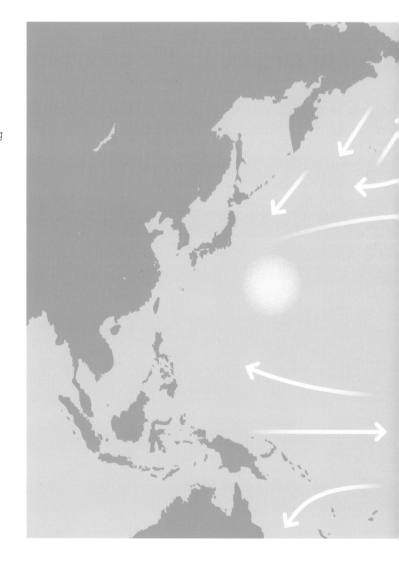

A chemical called polylactic acid (PLA) can be produced by removing starch from potatoes or corn. The long strings of sugars in starch are broken down into simpler units called dextrose, which is fed to microbes and converted to lactic acid in fermentation. Lastly, the lactic acid is connected into long chains of PLA, which can be stored as small pellets. Not only is PLA made from things we can grow, bacteria can make a meal of it quickly and easily. This might make it unsuitable for some things, but for packaging that has a short life or can only be used once, it could help save our oceans from a lot of mess.

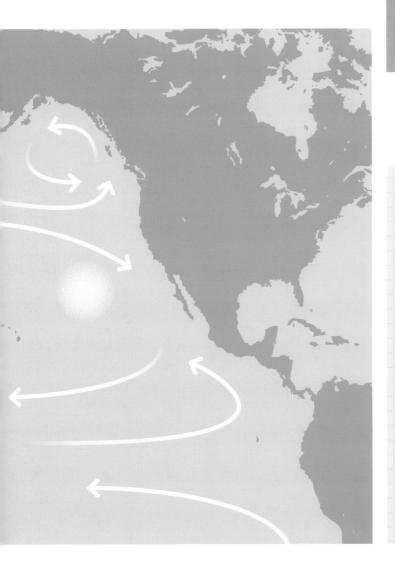

ANSWER THIS

1. What is the term of long strings of single chemical units?

2. What natural resource is most plastic produced from?

3. What are the two major methods for recycling plastics?

4. Why can't some plastics be recycled?

FERTILE GROUNDS

All living things need the right chemicals in their diet to build bodies. Animals get most of their fats, sugars, amino acids, vitamins, and minerals from materials they consume and digest. Plants can make sugars from water, carbon dioxide, and a bit of sunlight, but other building blocks need to be absorbed from the soil. This includes a good supply of nitrogen to make proteins.

By the middle of the Industrial Revolution, the world's population was beginning to swell in numbers. Farmers would once feed their crops nitrogen in the form of fertilizers made from waste, such as discarded animal bodies and even human sewage. With increasing demand for food, they simply couldn't get enough nitrogen for their fields. Finally, an answer came at the dawn of the 20th century, when a German chemist managed to turn the nitrogen in the air into a form that could be useful for everything from growing crops to making weapons.

Fixing the nitrogen problem

Nitrogen in the air takes the form of a molecule made of two nitrogen atoms. While roughly 80 percent of our atmosphere is made up of this molecule, it doesn't react (or "fix") very easily with other elements. This is why plants can't simply soak it up and use it to make more plant cells.

The chemist Fritz Haber discovered he could cause nitrogen to react with hydrogen gas to make ammonia by using a catalyst. While the catalyst made the gases react quickly, it also required a lot of heat, which also cased the ammonia to break down again rather rapidly. To get around this dilemma, Haber squeezed the whole reaction under a huge amount of pressure. This made it harder for the big ammonia molecules to break down into two smaller molecules, allowing enough ammonia to build up that the process could be used on an industrial scale. The Haber process produced ample amounts of ammonia from hydrogen and atmospheric nitrogen, which could then be used to make more than enough fertilizer for farmers. It also provided Germany with a key ingredient for explosives during a crucial period in World War I.

THE HABER PROCESS

1. Hydrogen (H₂) and nitrogen (N₂) gas enter a reactor with an iron-based metal that speeds up the reaction.

2. The resulting ammonia (NH₃) is put under pressure and cooled, where it condenses.

Some of the ammonia reacts to form nitrogen and hydrogen again. These are recycled.

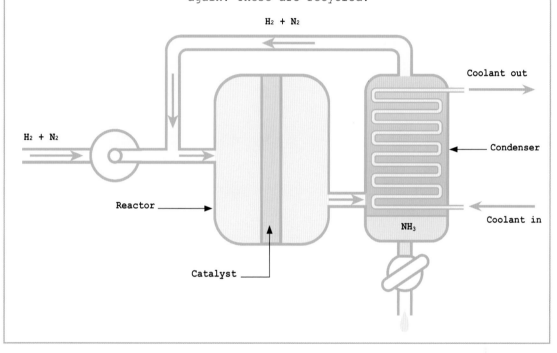

$H_2 + N_2$

$H_2 + N_2$

Coolant out

Condenser

Reactor

Coolant in

NH_3

Catalyst

ANSWER THIS

1. Where do plants get the nitrogen they need to make proteins?

2. How did farmers provide their crops with enough nitrogen for growth?

3. How much of the atmosphere is made up of nitrogen gas?

4. How did Fritz Haber create ammonia?

5. Ammonia was used to make fertilizer. What else can it be used to make?

ENGINEERING AND SPORTS

Strong competition in sports means engineering plays a central role in pushing the limits of human strength, speed, power, and endurance by coming up with better materials and structures. In doing so, engineers have changed how sports are played, raising questions of where the line between a fair competition and unfair advantage is drawn.

ENGINEERED EQUIPMENT

SWIMMING
Textured hydrophobic (water-"hating") fabrics that disrupt the flowing water can now be tailored to fit individual swimmers, helping muscles move in ways that increase their efficiency.

SOCCER BALL
Leather might be tough enough to handle a good beating, but it absorbs water and deforms over time. Vulcanized rubber invented back in the early 1800s by Charles Goodyear has led to balls that keep their shape better and won't grow heavy with water.

GOLF
When air slides over a moving ball's surface, it slips away from the curved rear and separates smoothly, leaving a small "turbulent wake region." The pressure inside this area pulls on the ball, creating drag. Adding dimples over the surface of a golf ball makes air flowing over the ball take longer to separate, so the turbulent wake region is smaller, and the ball travels farther.

CYCLING

To make a bicycle that can move faster, engineers need to overcome three challenges: resistance of moving parts, resistance of the rolling wheels, and resistance of the air. Making bicycles from lighter materials such as carbon fiber and eliminating parts that aren't completely necessary, which includes the brakes, has helped to make them easier to accelerate. Computational fluid dynamics tools are used by engineers to map the flow of air around a bicycle and rider to find areas they can tweak for faster rides.

RUNNING

About two and a half times of a runner's body weight is transferred onto the shoe every time the foot hits the ground. When the ground pushes back, this force can slow movement and shock bones and muscles. That means to help improve running, engineers focus on making shoes that can handle heavy steps. This means designing shoes that conform to the feet while giving them room to move naturally.

CHEMICAL ENGINEERING

1. **What was a common goal of early alchemists?**

   a. To transform base metals into gold

   b. To bake the perfect cake

   c. To discover the periodic table of elements

   d. To make gunpowder

2. **What distinguishes alchemists from chemical engineers?**

   a. Alchemists never invented anything

   b. Alchemists didn't apply their discoveries to improve anything

   c. Alchemists never wrote anything down

   d. Alchemists were less scientific in their explanations and experiments

3. **What form do metals often take in nature?**

   a. Mixes of molecules called salts

   b. Mixes of elements called compounds

   c. Mixes of minerals called ores

   d. Mixes of metals called alloys

4. **Why is gold often found in its elemental (pure) form in nature?**

   a. Gold is too rare to be found as an ore

   b. Gold smelts at very low temperatures

   c. Gold is too hard to break down

   d. Gold doesn't react easily with other elements

5. **One of the oldest metal artifacts was found in Israel in 2007. When was it thought to have been made?**

   a. About 10,200 BC

   b. About 5200 BC

   c. About 200 BC

   d. About 1200 BC

6. **Which color pigment was made from squashed cochineal bugs?**

   a. Green

   b. Blue

   c. Black

   d. Red

7. **What do all plastics have in common?**

   a. Plastics are all made from oil

   b. Plastics are all carbon-based polymers

   c. Plastics are all dangerous to wildlife

   d. Plastics are all made from polyethylene terephthalate (PET)

8. **Engineers are working on a family of plastics that aren't made from oil or break down easily in the environment. What are these plastics called?**

   a. Bioplastics

   b. Potato plastics

   c. Polylactic acid plastics

   d. Super plastics

Answers on page 216

SIMPLE SUMMARY

Chemical engineering involves the application of physics, biology, and chemistry to develop new and better materials that are more suited for a specific task.

- Early alchemy practices involved mixing solutions in order to turn "imperfect" mixes of elements into perfect ones—the most perfect of all being gold.

- The practice of using heat and carbon to separate a metal such as copper out from the mix of elements making up its ore is called smelting.

- Colored chemicals called pigments emit color by soaking up, or absorbing, wavelengths from the mix of radiation in white light. What they don't absorb bounces back out, which we see as color.

- One thing we can all do to minimize plastic waste is to reduce, reuse, and recycle.

- Bioplastics are a family of materials based on carbon polymers that aren't made from oil, or can easily break down in the environment.

- The chemist Fritz Haber discovered he could cause nitrogen to react with hydrogen gas to make ammonia by using a catalyst.

- Engineers have changed how sports are played, raising questions of where the line between a fair competition and unfair advantage is drawn.

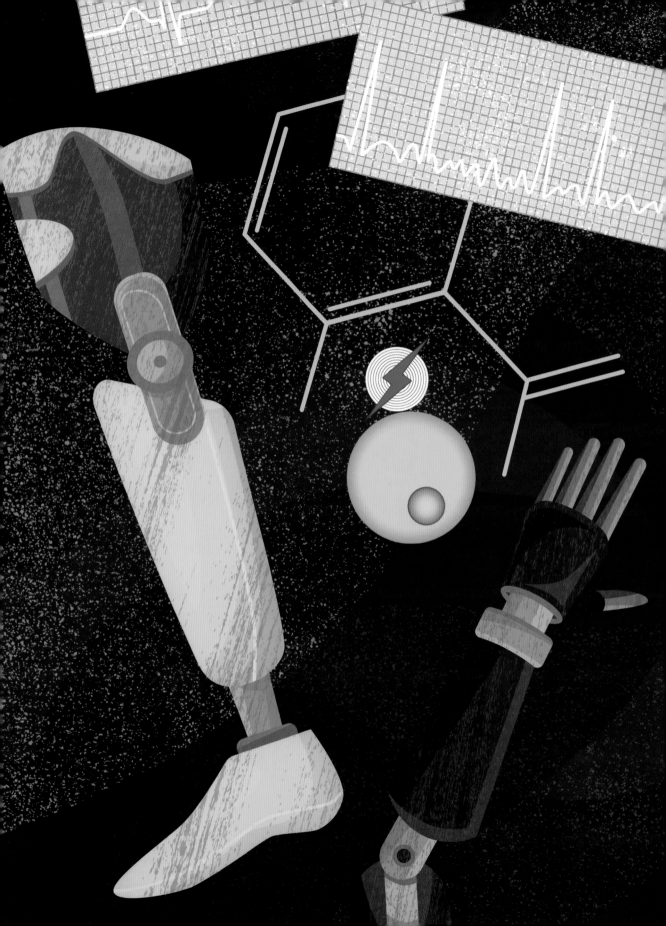

8

BIOENGINEERING

The human body can be compared to a complex machine. Bones and muscles work like levers; the cardiovascular system pumps liquids through a network of pipes; even on a microscopic level, cells burn fuel like molecular engines. So when it fails, engineers step in to use what they know about chemistry and physics to fix our biology. Just imagine how we might repair and improve our bodies with bioengineering in the future!

WHAT YOU WILL LEARN

Pharmaceutical engineering

I heart engineering

Getting under your skin

The body builders

How does your organ grow?

A baby in the lab

Engineering genes

An engineer in the kitchen

LESSON

8.1 PHARMACEUTICAL ENGINEERING

Sickness and disease are an unfortunate part of being alive. Bones break, microbes invade, and organs fail, making survival a struggle. Many animals learn that eating the right materials helps their bodies heal that little bit faster from the effects of illness.

Since the late 19th century, we've been able to identify, extract, and even manufacture the key healing components of natural materials like never before. Today, the production of medicines is a global industry worth around $1 trillion.

Chemists find potential new ways to treat illness in many different areas. Some come from natural ecosystems such as rainforests or coral reefs, which have often been used by local indigenous cultures for generations. Others are created by producing computer models of our body's chemistry and working backward, either using computers to modify existing treatments, or singling them out by trial and error.

FACT

Drug design can start with predicting the shapes of molecules in the body. In 2008 the University of Washington turned the challenge into a computer game called Foldit, where players had to figure out how amino acids were arranged into proteins.

Ehrlich's magic bullet

By the dawn of the 20th century, scientists were discovering that many diseases were caused by infections of microscopic organisms. While the organisms could be poisoned, the challenge was to find drugs that didn't also poison the patient. The German physician Paul Ehrlich imagined a chemical "magic bullet" that could "shoot" a microbe without harming the body around it. He and his researchers tested hundreds of similar compounds made from another drug called Atoxyl, which had recently been considered too toxic for people to use.

In 1909 they found a "bullet" that could kill a bacterium responsible for the disease syphilis, called *Treponema pallidum*. Sold under the name Salvarsan, it was far better than previous toxic treatments of mercury, and would be one of the world's best "magic bullets" until the isolation and production of penicillin more than 30 years later.

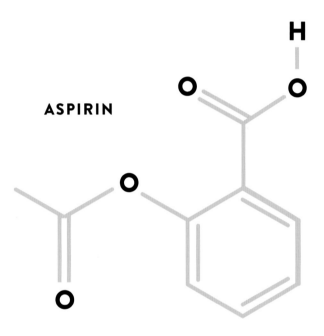

ASPIRIN

In 1853 the chemist Charles Frédéric Gerhardt added acetyl chloride to a salt of a plant compound called salicylic acid. While the acid had been used in medicine for centuries, this new version was less irritating. It was later sold as aspirin.

ANSWER THIS

1. How do animals help their bodies heal?

2. What was Salvarsan?

3. What could Ehrlich's "magic bullet" do?

4. Where can chemists find new materials on which to base pharmaceuticals?

5. How much is the global pharmaceutical industry worth?

LESSON
8.2 I HEART ENGINEERING

When another person's life is in your hands, it's vital that his blood keeps moving oxygen around his body. At its most basic, this could simply involve performing chest compressions until help arrives. Even the most experienced of doctors need a helping hand from devices that keep us alive until our organs are well enough to take care of themselves.

In spite of what you've seen in Hollywood movies, the "heart-starting" machines called defibrillators aren't used to start hearts at all. They're actually used to reset hearts that aren't pumping as rhythmically as they should be.

Heart muscle coordinates its cells to pulse using waves of charged particles, called ions, moving in and out of nerve and muscle cells. When this pulse gets messy, an electric current sent between two appropriately positioned poles—the "paddles" on a defibrillator—can force the tissues to depolarize. This causes the flow of those atoms to halt and settle into positions that allow the entire heart to reset and pump rhythmically again. This was first demonstrated in 1899 by two Swiss doctors, who showed in dogs that a current could cause their hearts to "fibrillate," or quiver. A second, larger shock could then cause defibrillation, helping the heart beat normally again.

MADE SIMPLE
ECG

The first illustration is an electrocardiogram reading of a healthy heart rhythm. The second is a heart in atrial fibrillation, squeezing blood out in an uncoordinated fashion, which does a poor job of moving it around the body.

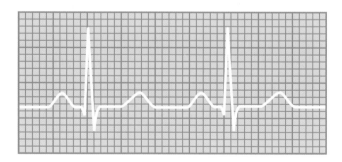

NORMAL ECG

Pacemakers

In rare instances, an engineering mistake can serve as an inspiration for history-changing inventions. That's exactly what happened to the American physician Wilson Greatbatch, who in 1956 set out to make something that could record the heart's rhythm, but made a crucial error. When Greatbatch constructed the circuit, he accidentally inserted a transistor 100 times more powerful than the one he had planned for. This component amplified electrical signals, turning a simple recorder into a tiny device that emitted pulses of electricity in a rhythm that mimicked those of a healthy human heart.

Four years later, Greatbatch's artificial pacemaker was implanted into a patient along with batteries to keep it ticking for five years. There were other electronics that could also spark a weak heart with occasional pulses of electricity, but most were too large to wear, or just plain unreliable. Greatbatch's "mistake" has saved millions of lives around the world for more than half a century.

ANSWER THIS

1. What do Hollywood movies get wrong about "heart-stopping" moments using a defibrillator?

2. What causes heart muscle to coordinate contractions?

3. What is a heart doing when fibrillating?

4. What device did the physician Wilson Greatbatch set out to make in 1956?

5. What device did Greatbatch eventually introduce in 1960?

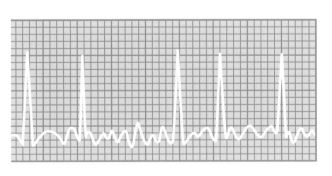

ATRIAL FIBRILLATION

LESSON 8.3

GETTING UNDER YOUR SKIN

Skin does a tremendously good job of keeping your squishy bits moist and free of germs. It also happens to make it impossible to take a good look at the state of your organs, bones, and other tissues. When things go wrong, doctors need to make use of specially designed tools to peek inside your body.

In 1895 a German mechanical engineer named Wilhelm Röntgen noticed that a tube containing a small amount of gas caused a nearby fluorescent sheet of paper to light up when a current passed through it, even while covered with paper. He had discovered a new kind of light that could pass through certain materials. This led to a device that would make and send these special "X-rays" through a body and onto film. Since the rays were blocked by bones, it became one of the first tools for photographing the skeleton.

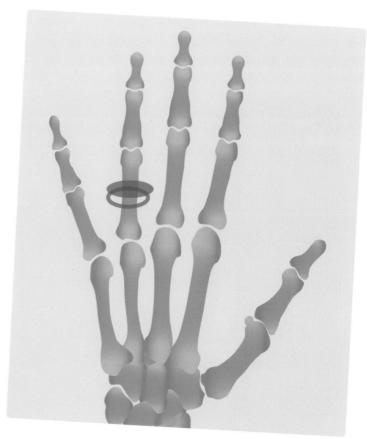

X-RAYS

The first ever X-ray image of a human bone was of Röntgen's wife's left hand, complete with her wedding ring. She was so shocked she is said to have exclaimed, "I have seen my death!"

Magnetic resonance imaging (MRI)

Inside the nucleus of every atom in your body there's one or more positively charged particles called protons. These particles can be forced to line up inside a super-strong magnetic field, a little like tiny compass needles pointing north. Under the dull glow of radio waves, the protons all jiggle and turn in slightly different ways. As soon as the radio signal stops, the protons emit a burst of energy as they snap back into position. Sensors read these bursts as differences in the body's chemistry, safely providing a detailed image of your insides.

Ultrasound

If you've ever heard a conversation in the next room, you'll know sound can go where light can't travel. You might also know that the way sound waves bend and echo gives you a sense of a room's space and objects. Super-short ultrasound waves are too high-pitched for human ears to detect. They can be made thanks to a discovery by French chemist Pierre Curie, who found that special "piezoelectric" materials could vibrate rapidly when stimulated by electricity. In the 1940s, physicists used Curie's discovery in devices that could beam tiny sound waves into a human body, and turn their echo into an image. Today we use ultrasound devices for a range of medical reasons. In fact, your very first photograph could have been taken with one while you were still in the womb. Hope you said "cheese!"

ANSWER THIS

1. What kind of light did Wilhelm Röntgen discover in 1895?

2. What do the letters MRI stand for in medical imaging?

3. What happens to your body's protons when the flow of radio waves in an MRI machine stops?

4. Why can't humans hear ultrasound waves?

5. What is one common application for ultrasound scanning?

FACT

The first stethoscope was created by the French physician René Laennec in 1816. He used a dozen or so sheets of rolled-up paper to listen more clearly to the chest of a large woman. This inspired him to create a wooden cylinder to take on his rounds.

8.4 THE BODY BUILDERS

Losing a part of your body can be a traumatizing experience. Today, surgeons can often reattach fingers, limbs, or even facial features so that they can heal in place well enough to return some function. Where that isn't possible, technology can replicate many organs and structures, from arms and legs to eyes and ears, and even hearts and lungs. In some cases, they might even work nearly as well as the real thing.

The area of medicine that uses technology to replace body parts with synthetic materials is called prosthetics. Many different fields of engineering contribute to developing prosthetic devices, including electrical engineers, materials scientists, and bioengineers. Each lends its experience to make systems that move and respond to the person wearing it, without throwing the wearer off balance, making them uncomfortable, or taking too much effort to use. The earliest prosthetic device ever found dates back to between 710 and 950 BC. It was a big toe carved from wood and attached to leather straps, probably used to help its wearer walk comfortably.

FACT

Engineers are working on devices that can measure blood glucose levels and calculate how much insulin to deliver. With access to an artificial pancreas, a diabetic could rely on computer technology to do the work of a biological pancreas, reducing the risk of illness and even death from fluctuating sugar levels.

Breathing life

Breathing is an essential part of living. When the body can't manage this on its own, thanks to a failure of the heart or respiratory system, an extracorporeal membrane oxygenation (ECMO) can be applied. This involves taking blood from a large vein, usually near the thigh, and sending it through a machine that uses a special membrane to add oxygen without the need for the blood to come into direct contact with open air, similar to actual lungs. It's then warmed before being returned to the patient through another vein or artery.

ECMO was developed in the 1950s by American surgeon John Gibbon for long operations involving the heart and lungs. Previous machines had small chambers where blood could clot easily. Gibbon's method was simpler and safer, and is today used around the world to treat a wide variety of health conditions.

PROSTHETICS

Improvements to technology are making prosthetics lighter and stronger, with mechanisms for comfort and better control.

Prosthetic limbs come in many forms to suit a variety of functions and appearances.

ANSWER THIS

1. What field of medicine deals with using technology to create synthetic body parts?

2. What is the earliest example of a body part being replaced with a well-crafted copy?

3. Which body systems do extracorporeal membrane oxygenation (ECMO) do the job of?

4. What was the problem with the other machines that added oxygen to blood?

LESSON
8.5

HOW DOES YOUR ORGAN GROW?

Ever since the first successful blood transfusions were conducted in the early 19th century, physicians have continued to push the boundaries on transplanting different tissues, organs, and even limbs from a donor into somebody who desperately needs it.

Roughly 140,000 organ transplants are conducted each year in more than 60 countries around the globe. Nearly 8,000 of those organs are hearts, with most of the remaining transplants made up of either livers or kidneys. All organ transplants between different people run the risk of failing thanks to our immune system. Specialized white blood cells can detect even the smallest of differences in transplanted cells, alerting the body to attack. To prevent this, patients need to take powerful drugs that keep their immune system quiet enough to prevent the donated organ from being damaged.

FACT

Transplants aren't the only reason for growing tissues and organs in the lab. A burger made of lab-grown beef tissue was made by Maastricht University in the Netherlands in 2013. It cost $270,000, and took several months to grow. Recent attempts by other companies have now brought costs down to just under $110 a pound.

Bioengineers are investigating new ways to "grow" cells, tissues, and even whole organs that behave just like those in a patient's body. Some are already a reality; others, like the growing of functioning hearts and kidneys, could one day save the lives of millions.

Organ renovation

Every cell in your body carries the genetic blueprints to make every other cell, from nerves to muscles to even your blood. While most cells already have a clear job, some, called stem cells, are yet to take a clear form. One way bioengineers can construct body parts that your immune system won't reject is to start with a donated organ and remove as many of its own cells as possible. This leaves a stiff web of proteins that provide a scaffold for cells called an extracellular matrix, but won't alert the immune system. It's as if you've taken another person's house and stripped out the distinguishing carpet, fancy tiles, and colorful wall panels. Stem cells are used to replace the hardworking cells. By seeding the scaffold with these immature cells and bathing them in the right mix of nutrients and hormones, bioengineers can turn them into nearly any tissue. Once they cover the scaffold, the cells fully develop tissue the shape of the organ needed—one the body will treat as its very own.

PRINTED ORGANS?

Organs are made of many different types of tissue, each of which needs to grow in their own special place. One way we might be able to construct these in the future is by using a 3-D printer that can print a scaffold and seed it with the right kinds of cells.

ANSWER THIS

1. Why do organ transplants often fail?

2. What kind of cells can we use to turn into just about any tissue in the body?

3. What is the name of the stiff scaffold of proteins that help shape organs?

4. How many organ transplants take place around the world each year?

5. How much did the first laboratory-grown beef burger cost?

8.6 A BABY IN THE LAB

For some couples, starting a family can require a lot of patience. A lucky third will fall pregnant within the first month. Around 85 percent should fall pregnant within a year of first trying to conceive, but for roughly one in ten men and women, the opportunity to have a baby becomes vanishingly small.

Biotechnology offers many couples who can't easily fall pregnant a second chance at becoming biological parents. Assisted reproductive technology describes a range of procedures aimed at helping to fertilize an egg cell, or ovum, and turn it into a healthy newborn. In some cases, this simply involves delivering sperm into the mother's uterus, but some procedures can be a little more complicated.

In vitro fertilization (IVF) requires the mother to take hormones that will cause her body to release more ova than it would usually. These egg cells are collected in a surgical procedure and combined with sperm outside of the body. Once technicians are satisfied that at least one of the ova has been fertilized, the resulting embryo is transferred into the uterus. If more than one embryo forms, the remainder are preserved by freezing.

Mom, Dad, and . . .

Your body is the product of a random assortment of genes that came from two other humans we call biological parents. But in Mexico in 2016, a child was born who had a third human contribute to her genetic mix. Most cells in your body contain the bulk of their genetic material in a small pocket called a nucleus, but that's not the only bundle of DNA in your cell. There's a small amount of it inside the power supply for your cell—tiny cellular organs called mitochondria. All of your mitochondria came from one place—your mother's ovum. A genetic change in the mother's mitochondria's genes can carry a big risk of the disorder Leigh syndrome. So scientists found a way to take the nucleus from a mother's ova and swap it with the nucleus in a donor's healthier egg, helping mothers conceive healthy children.

MADE SIMPLE
CLONING

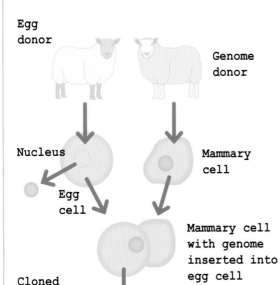

Egg donor

Genome donor

Nucleus

Mammary cell

Egg cell

Mammary cell with genome inserted into egg cell

Cloned cell shocked

Embryo contains cells with mammary cell's genome

Clone has same basic genetic code

A sheep named Dolly made history when she was born on July 5, 1995. She had the honor of being the first animal to be born as a clone. To create her, bioengineers took a cell from an adult sheep and removed its nucleus. This was placed into an egg cell from a second sheep which had its nucleus removed and discarded. A third sheep carried the embryo and gave birth.

ANSWER THIS

1. How many couples fall pregnant within the first year of trying to conceive?

2. What is IVF and how does it work?

3. Aside from the nucleus, where else would you find DNA in a cell?

4. Where do all of your mitochondria come from?

5. Why is Dolly the sheep so famous?

If your DNA was a series of books in a library, genes would be chapters full of instructions on how to perform a task. Some are recipes for proteins; others tell you how to read other chapters; a few even have pages missing, or letters rearranged so they don't make sense.

Since ancient times, farmers have grown the most nutritious crops and raised the woolliest, fattest, or strongest livestock by being picky about who gets to be a parent. This is called selective breeding. By selecting seeds from the choicest crops, or only allowing the best animals to breed, farmers were keeping "chapters" they wanted while letting others disappear. More recently, scientists have discovered there are bacteria that make proteins called enzymes which can be used to cut and rearrange specific sentences in a DNA library. By picking the right enzymes and using technology to sort the resulting mess of fallen pages into different sizes, genetic engineers can edit genes directly and even rearrange them to add the characteristics they want, while removing others. This can be used to insert genes for pharmaceuticals into bacteria, to remove disease-causing genes from livestock, or even to make crops more resistant to pests.

CRISPR-Cas9

In the late 1990s, scientists had found strange repeating sequences of DNA in bacteria called clustered regularly interspaced short palindromic repeats, or CRISPR. They discovered they contained genes stolen from viruses that had tried to infect the bacteria. Years later, their secret weapon was found—virus-killing enzymes that used these genes to "remember" past attackers. Those sequences and enzymes—called CRISPR-Cas9—are now used by genetic engineers to pinpoint DNA sequences they want to change in just about any cell. By spelling out part of a gene, they can send in an enzyme to make a cut, ruining the gene or making room for a new sequence.

Some researchers are concerned the technology isn't perfect enough to use on people yet. While it could be used to break genes that cause disease, it could make unwanted cuts in other genes, raising the risk that some cells might go haywire, causing cancer.

HOW CRISPR WORKS

A COPY OF THE TARGET GENETIC SEQUENCE is linked with an enzyme called Cas9.

Guide RNA

Cas9 enzyme

Cleavage

Repair

Insertion

THE ENZYME FINDS A MATCHING SEQUENCE in the cell's DNA.

CAS9 BREAKS THE TARGET DNA at a precise point. This either makes the gene unreadable or a new sequence can be glued in place to make a different gene.

ANSWER THIS

1. How would you describe a gene?

2. What is selective breeding?

3. What is genetic engineering used for?

4. What do bacteria use CRISPR-Cas9 for?

5. What could be some of the risks if we used CRISPR-Cas9 to treat disease in a living human?

AN ENGINEER IN THE KITCHEN

Behind just about every product in your local supermarket there's an engineering story. Sometimes it's to make the food taste better, make it look more appealing, or to make sure it stays fresh. In some cases, new technology is used, but often it's an old trick that's been around for centuries.

Food technology has become more important in modern times for feeding greater numbers of people while making products safer. Yet humans have been preserving meat and vegetables since ancient times, protecting it from microbes by removing moisture and adding antimicrobial agents. One way this has traditionally been done is through drying, salting, or smoking. With less water available, microorganisms in the environment have a harder time moving through the food and reproducing. Particles in the salt and smoke help draw out more moisture while creating a hostile environment that makes it harder for germs to survive.

FACT
Many foods you might think of as sweet, such as bread and breakfast cereal, could contain surprisingly high amounts of salt to enhance flavor. This hidden sodium makes it harder to keep salt levels down.

MADE SIMPLE
COMMON FOOD ADDITIVES FROM NATURAL SOURCES

E120
Cochineal: red coloring
Cochineal insect

E260
Acetic acid:
preserving agent
Vinegar

E322
Lecithin: emulsifier
(helps fats mix with water)
In egg yolks

What's your number?

Today, chemical engineers will often add materials to food to make it look, feel, or taste more appetizing, sometimes by adding color or preventing it from reacting with oxygen. While some have complicated names, many are found naturally in fruits or spices, or as common ingredients. For example, vitamin C, found in citrus fruits, can be added to help soak up oxygen that could ruin a food's color. To make it easier to keep track of them, these additives are given an "E" number that places them into categories such as colors, preservatives, thickening agents, or sweeteners. The "E" stands for Europe, though the numbers are also used in other countries.

Over the years, people have been concerned about the inclusion of some specific chemicals in food, such as coloring agents amaranth (E123) and tartrazine (E102). While some additives risk reactions in people with allergies, there's little scientific evidence that any are considered to be widely toxic or dangerous in reasonable amounts.

ANSWER THIS

1. How did people preserve food in ancient times?

2. What does smoking do to meat to help keep it from rotting?

3. Why do food engineers add vitamin C to some foods?

4. What does the "E" stand for in E-numbers?

E401
Sodium alginate: thickener
In algae

E904
Shellac: glazing agent
From the lac bug

BIOENGINEERING

1. One of the first antibiotics to be developed was sold as Salvarsan. What illness did it treat?

   a. Tuberculosis

   b. Syphilis

   c. Golden staph

   d. Measles

2. What does a defibrillator machine do?

   a. Stops a quivering heart

   b. Starts a stopped heart

   c. Makes a slow heartbeat faster

   d. Brings people back to life

3. What lifesaving device did Wilson Greatbatch's "mistake" lead to in 1960?

   a. The defibrillator

   b. X-ray machines

   c. The wearable pacemaker

   d. Resuscitation mannequins

4. How do magnetic resonance imaging machines map your body's tissues?

   a. By listening to your body's radio waves

   b. By measuring the X-rays inside your body

   c. By measuring which atoms in your body point north

   d. By measuring changes in the atoms' protons in a magnetic field

5. The earliest known prosthetic device was a large wooden toe. When was it thought to have been made?

   a. Between 10,000 and 9500 BC

   b. Between 950 and 710 BC

   c. Between 100 and 50 BC

   d. Between 1850 and 1910

6. In bioengineering, what is a stem cell?

   a. A cell that carries water inside a plant

   b. A cell found only inside the brain

   c. A cell that is yet to develop features for a specific task

   d. An artificial cell made in the laboratory

7. What percentage of couples have a relatively small chance of conceiving at all?

   a. About 1 percent

   b. About 10 percent

   c. About 25 percent

   d. About 50 percent

8. Why do chemical engineers add materials to food?

   a. To follow the law

   b. To speed up the manufacturing process

   c. To make it look, feel, or taste more appetizing

   d. To cure diabetes

Answers on page 217

SIMPLE SUMMARY

When the human body fails, engineers step in to use what they know about chemistry and physics to fix our biology.

- Since the late 19th century, we've been able to identify, extract, and even manufacture the key healing components of natural materials like never before.

- Defibrillators are used to reset hearts that aren't pumping as rhythmically as they should be.

- In 1895, Wilhelm Röntgen discovered a new kind of light that could pass through certain materials, which led to the invention of X-rays.

- The area of medicine that uses technology to replace body parts with synthetic materials is called prosthetics.

- Roughly 140,000 organ transplants are conducted each year in more than 60 countries around the globe.

- Assisted reproductive technology describes a range of procedures aimed at helping to fertilize an egg cell, or ovum, and turn it into a healthy newborn.

- Scientists have discovered there are bacteria that make proteins called enzymes, which can be used to cut and rearrange specific sentences in a DNA library.

- Food technology has become more important in modern times for feeding greater numbers of people while making products safer.

9

COMMUNICATIONS

We think nothing of communicating instantly with somebody halfway across the world, but only 200 years ago it would have taken weeks to send a message that far. The invention of electricity finally allowed instant long-distance communication through the telegraph, the telephone, radio, and television, but we are far more connected now, thanks to advances in computing and the Internet. We now share our ideas more than at any other point in history.

WHAT YOU WILL LEARN

Communications past

Waves of communication

Going digital

A world of data

COMMUNICATIONS PAST

Humans are a chatty bunch. Exactly when our ancestors developed speech isn't clear, but roughly half a million years ago, primates evolved ways to communicate ideas through sounds produced by moving their lips, tongues, and throat. And we haven't shut up since!

This talent is what we call modality-independent. It means the format of the ideas doesn't matter—we can say "hello" out loud, or we can wave, or write the word down in symbols, and our brains will still know it's a greeting. So for 10,000 years or so, humans have represented ideas by scratching them down using symbolic images or words. Writing is useful for sending thoughts across long distances and preserving ideas to future generations. In 1439, a German metalsmith named Johannes Gutenberg came up with an invention that would transform the way humans communicate.

Gutenberg developed a quick and easy way to produce uniform sets of letters that could be arranged in a frame to create a unique "stamp" to press out typed pages. His printing press was a lot faster than other ways of pressing out pages, and certainly quicker than handwriting. Books could be made in vast numbers at low cost; it was a writing revolution!

Ring ring!

Along the Great Wall of China there are towers where large fires once burned. To send a signal down the wall, people would watch for a distant flame and set their kindling alight, alerting people farther down the wall to do the same.

Sending a message over distant horizons is a lot easier today, thanks in part to early electrical engineers in the 18th and 19th centuries. By tinkering with ways to send patterns of electrical current through a conductor, they determined it was possible to communicate a message from one end of a wire to the other. The problem is, long wires have high resistance, which makes it difficult to pass a current through. In 1828, American scientist Joseph Henry strengthened electromagnets so a weak current could produce a stronger magnetic pulse. He used this in 1831 to ring a bell by sending a current down a 1-mile (1.6-kilometer) long wire. This kick-started the technology that gave rise to the modern world of electric telecommunication devices.

MORSE CODE

Early electronic communication could only make use of
a current that could be turned completely on or off.
An inventor of the first telegraph, Samuel Morse, used this
on-off pattern to create a code that could be sent along a
wire. His first version was only numbers, which could be
used to identify words in a codebook. It was expanded in the
1840s to communicate an entire alphabet.

A	• ▬	**J**	• ▬ ▬ ▬	**S**	• • •	**1**	• ▬ ▬ ▬ ▬
B	▬ • • •	**K**	▬ • ▬	**T**	▬	**2**	• • ▬ ▬ ▬
C	▬ • ▬ •	**L**	• ▬ • •	**U**	• • ▬	**3**	• • • ▬ ▬
D	▬ • •	**M**	▬ ▬	**V**	• • • ▬	**4**	• • • • ▬
E	•	**N**	▬ •	**W**	• ▬ ▬	**5**	• • • • •
F	• • ▬ •	**O**	▬ ▬ ▬	**X**	▬ • • ▬	**6**	▬ • • • •
G	▬ ▬ •	**P**	• ▬ ▬ •	**Y**	▬ • ▬ ▬	**7**	▬ ▬ • • •
H	• • • •	**Q**	▬ ▬ • ▬	**Z**	▬ ▬ • •	**8**	▬ ▬ ▬ • •
I	• •	**R**	• ▬ •			**9**	▬ ▬ ▬ ▬ •
						0	▬ ▬ ▬ ▬ ▬

1. The length of a dot is one unit.
2. A dash is three units.
3. The space between parts of the same letter is one unit.
4. The space between letters is three units.
5. The space between words is seven units.

ANSWER THIS

1. Approximately when did our primate ancestors begin to use true speech to communicate?

2. What did Johannes Gutenberg develop in 1439?

3. In what decade was Morse code expanded to communicate the entire alphabet?

4. What letter does a single dot represent in Morse code?

WAVES OF COMMUNICATION

The American engineer Alexander Graham Bell was a man of vision. Credited with inventing what he called an "electrical speech machine," he once claimed that every city in America would have one. If only he were alive today to see just how many people would own one of his famous inventions!

The telephone started with telegraphs sent by interrupting a current, producing a digital "on-off" pattern for coded messages. To transmit something as complex as speech, Bell needed to send a signal that was more complex. His invention turned waves of sound into changes in a current, which turned back into vibrations that could form sound again. Early versions of his ideas could turn a voice into garbled noises, but they couldn't clearly carry the details of spoken words.

In 1876, Bell tested a device called a liquid transmitter. It was a needle that dangled from a thin skin drum into a conducting fluid. Sounds made the skin vibrate, which shook the needle and caused the fluid to ripple. This caused the resistance in a circuit to fluctuate, sending a signal as a current of electricity. At the other end, a reverse process could cause another membrane to re-create sound waves. When Bell tested his device, he is said to have called for his assistant, saying, "Mr. Watson, come here. I want to see you."

FACT

Bell tried to sell his telephone patent to the telegraph company Western Union for just $100,000. They turned him down, making one of the biggest business mistakes in history.

Cutting the wires

Stand outside in bright daylight and your skin would feel warm, as light from the sun heated your body. That white light would be made up of all the colors of the rainbow woven together. It would also contain colors we can't see—there would be a few high-energy, high-frequency X-rays; a generous dose of ultraviolet; a scattering of infrared; and further down the spectrum, a glow of microwaves and radio waves.

OPTICAL FIBERS

Electricity is just one way to send information long distances. Data can also be stored as a frequency, such as a color of light. Light waves can travel through a material by the process of total internal reflection. When waves pass from a medium of one density into a less-dense medium, they bend away from an imaginary perpendicular called the normal.

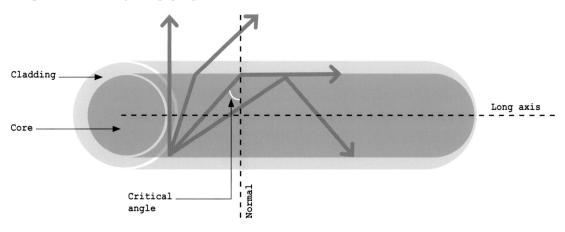

Scottish mathematician James Clerk Maxwell predicted the existence of low-energy radio waves in the 1860s, but it wasn't until 1886 that a German physicist named Heinrich Rudholph Hertz showed they existed. Meanwhile, engineers around the world were finding ways to transmit electromagnetic signals that were formed by electrical currents. It was slowly becoming clear that some sort of electrical signal could be used to send communications across gaps without a wire.

Italian engineer Guglielmo Marconi was among the first to accomplish this feat. Inspired by Hertz's discoveries, he used similar equipment to that used by the physicist to create what were then called Hertzian waves, which he used to send a signal across a space to cause a bell to ring on a separate circuit. By the turn of the century, Marconi's work on transmitting signals by electromagnetic radiation had come on in leaps and bounds. In 1901, he sent a signal bouncing across the Atlantic. It was just three dots—the letter "S" in Morse code.

ANSWER THIS

1. What's another name for Alexander Graham Bell's "electrical speech machine"?

2. What device did Bell first put to use in 1876 to convert sound into electrical signals?

3. What did Guglielmo Marconi famously send across the Atlantic in 1901?

9.3 GOING DIGITAL

A smartphone combines the jobs of a telephone, a telegraph, a library, a camera, a television, a music recorder and player, a radio, and a post office—and that is still just a fraction of the things that it can do. This is possible because of digital communications. By translating information into a binary code, computers could be integrated, making communications faster and more convenient, bringing us into the Information Age.

In 1689, Gottfried Leibniz realized that all numbers—and therefore all information—could be represented as a series of ones and zeros. However, he had no idea what his binary code could be used for. His idea, 250 years later, was used to program computers during World War II to crack codes—and modern computing was born.

MADE SIMPLE
ANALOG VS. DIGITAL

When communication signals are sent, they can get distorted and damaged as they go, creating "noise." When an analog signal is amplified, the noise is amplified too. Since digital signals have only two values, on and off, any noise can be ignored and the signal maintains its quality.

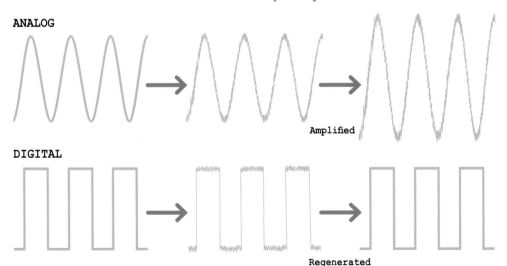

ANALOG

Amplified

DIGITAL

Regenerated

When sound is picked up by a microphone, the vibrations of air vibrate the microphone, and that vibration is turned into a continual electrical signal. When that signal goes to a speaker, the electrical signal produces vibrations in the speaker, re-creating the original sound that went into the microphone. This is an analog signal. If the signal is disturbed in any way, the output will be disturbed too.

The sound can also be represented digitally in binary code. The analog signal is chopped into pieces that last for a tiny fraction of a second, and each piece can be given values for its pitch and volume. These values can be represented in binary code and imprinted as a code on a CD or stored in a computer. The code can then be transformed back into an analog signal to reproduce the sound through a speaker.

One advantage of this is that slight disturbances in the signal can be corrected and so signals can be sent farther without losing any quality. They can also be sent through fiber optics using light, which is faster and more efficient than with electricity. Digital information can also be stored in computers instead of books and records, which is why you can now have an entire library of music, movies, books, and photos in your pocket.

ANSWER THIS

1. What is binary code?

2. What is an analog signal?

3. How is a digital signal for music created?

4. Give an advantage of sending digital signals.

5. Give an advantage of digital information storage.

LESSON
9.4 A WORLD OF DATA

In the early 1960s, computer scientists realized that if computers could talk to each other from a long distance, it would be easier to share information. The U.S. Department of Defense was the first to do this with ARPANET, and in 1969 the three letters L, O, and G were sent between two California universities, before the system crashed. There are now billions of interconnected computers on the Internet, and the idea has completely revolutionized communication and our day-to-day lives.

Throughout the 1970s and 1980s, networks sprang up between research institutes around the world, which eventually merged to form the global Internet. In 1989, Tim Berners-Lee, a computer scientist at CERN, a nuclear research institute, came up with the idea of being able to access information by following hyperlinks to particular pages where the information is stored. He called it the World Wide Web, and soon after developed the first web server and the first web browser.

Throughout the 1990s, home computers became more common and the Internet became somewhere to sell items, host bulletin boards, and communicate through email and in chat forums. As more people joined the Internet, it became useful for more and more things, and by the early 21st century, it was used for music sharing, social media, maps, and everything else we use it for today.

The next stage of the Internet will be the Internet of Things, where everyday objects, such as fridges, cars, and even pacemakers could be connected. If, say, millions of fridges could have their power turned down a fraction at the touch of a button, it could save power when the electricity grid is experiencing high demand. Connecting cars could help with traffic control, and Internet-connected pacemakers could send information on a patient's heart straight to their doctor.

WHERE IS THE INTERNET?

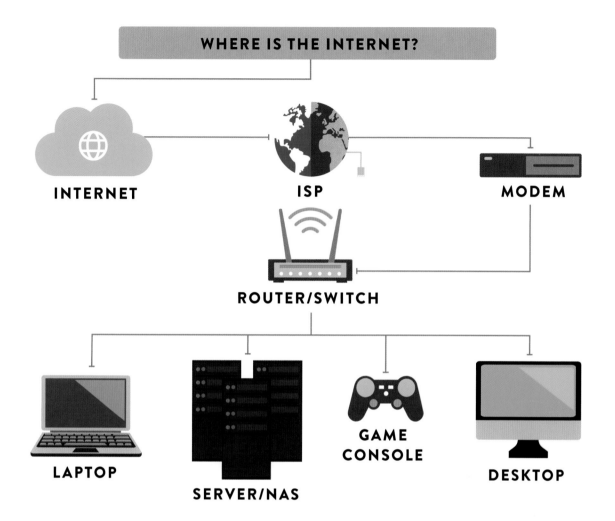

INTERNET

ISP

MODEM

ROUTER/SWITCH

LAPTOP

SERVER/NAS

GAME CONSOLE

DESKTOP

Every piece of information on the Internet is stored and processed somewhere on a server, and there are many of these spread all around the world. When you access a web page, a Wi-Fi signal from your phone or computer goes to your router, which sends the signal through fiber-optic cables or telephone wires out to your Internet service provider. The signal is then sent to the server holding the web page, which then sends a signal back.

ANSWER THIS

1. What was the first long-distance computer network?

2. What did Tim Berners-Lee invent?

3. What will be the next phase of the Internet?

4. What is a server?

5. Why has the smartphone allowed the Internet to grow so fast?

COMMUNICATIONS

1. How much data does an mp3 of a song contain?
   a. 35 megabytes
   b. 35 gigabytes
   c. 3.5 million bytes
   d. 3.5 billion gigabytes

2. Which one of the following was *not* an advantage of the printing press?
   a. It was faster than writing
   b. It could print detailed, full-color pictures
   c. Books could be made in large numbers
   d. It cost very little to print books

3. How were signals sent quickly along the length of the Great Wall of China?
   a. Electric telegraph
   b. Fires were lit
   c. Carrier pigeon
   d. Shouting

4. Who invented the telephone?
   a. Michael Faraday
   b. Marie Curie
   c. Alexander Graham Bell
   d. Alessandro Volta

5. What is a radio wave?
   a. A low-energy light wave
   b. A high-energy sound wave
   c. A high-energy light wave
   d. A low-energy sound wave

6. A Wi-Fi signal from your phone or computer goes to what first?
   a. Router
   b. Server
   c. Telephone mast
   d. Satellite

7. What are the two ways in which information can be stored and transferred?
   a. Fast and slow
   b. Analog and digital
   c. Light and sound
   d. High and low

8. When did Gottfried Liebniz invent binary code?
   a. 1200 BC
   b. 1250
   c. 1689
   d. 1947

9. What major innovation in communications was developed by Tim Berners-Lee at CERN in 1989?
   a. World Wide Web
   b. Telephone
   c. Smartphone
   d. Internet

10. What is the name of a machine that stores and processes websites?
    a. Storer
    b. Web browser
    c. Warehouse
    d. Server

Answers on page 218

SIMPLE SUMMARY

The invention of electricity finally allowed instant long-distance communication through the telegraph, the telephone, radio, and television, but we are far more connected now, thanks to advances in computing and the Internet.

- In 1439, a German metalsmith named Johannes Gutenberg invented the printing press, enabling books to be made in vast numbers at low cost.

- In 1876, Alexander Graham Bell tested a device called a liquid transmitter. It was a needle that dangled from a thin skin drum into a conducting fluid, and would come to be known as the first telephone.

- James Clerk Maxwell predicted the existence of low-energy radio waves in the 1860s, but it wasn't until 1886 that a German physicist named Heinrich Hertz showed they existed.

- In 1689, Gottfried Leibniz realized that all numbers could be represented as a series of ones and zeros—binary code; 250 years later, modern computing was born.

- In 1989, Tim Berners-Lee came up with the idea of being able to access information by following hyperlinks to particular pages where the information is stored. He called it the World Wide Web.

- The next stage of the Internet will be the Internet of Things, where everyday objects such as fridges, cars, and even pacemakers could be connected.

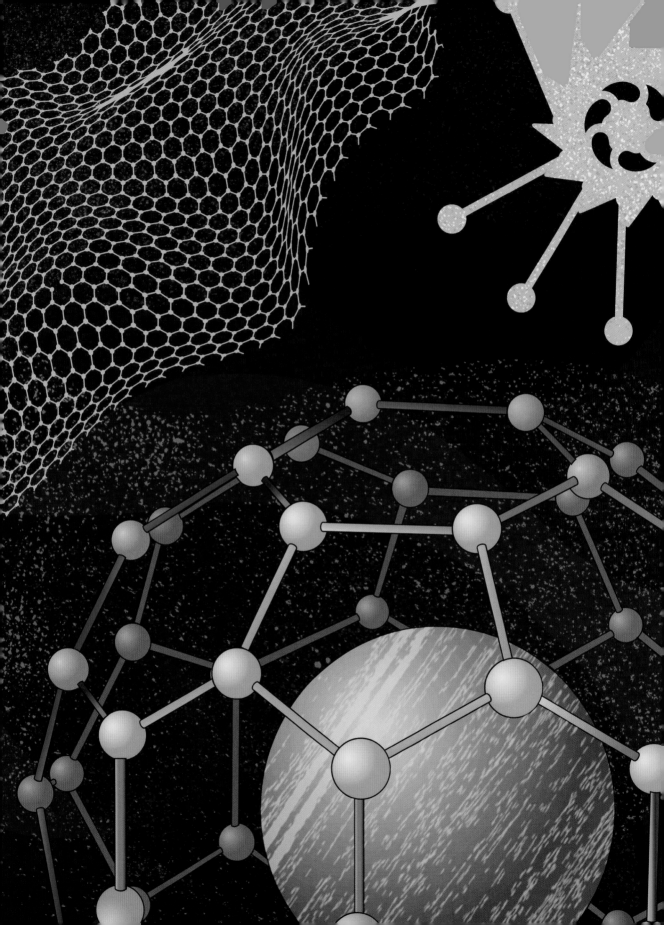

10
FUTURE ENGINEERING

History is full of examples of engineering marvels. As we learn more about how the universe works, technology will continue to overcome challenges to make stronger materials, more powerful machines, and faster electronics. Today's dreamers will become tomorrow's engineers, taking us to the stars and maybe beyond. Who knows, maybe you'll be the engineer who gets us there!

WHAT YOU WILL LEARN

Reaching for the stars

Asteroid engineering

Going smaller

Building new worlds

Impossible engineering?

10.1 REACHING FOR THE STARS

Standing outside, looking up at the night sky, it's easy to be overwhelmed by the number of stars—but it's just a fraction of what's out there. The farthest star we can see with the naked eye is a little more than 16,000 light-years away. The Milky Way is 100,000 light-years across, and it's just one of billions of galaxies in the universe!

Discovering all we can about distant objects in space will require some clever engineering. Wider telescopes, faster probes, and more intelligent robots are just the beginning—future engineers will need to come up with technology we can barely even dream of today.

FACT

The only technology to leave our solar system has been the two *Voyager* probes. Both left Earth in 1977 and took more than 30 years to reach the edge. If it was headed toward our nearest neighbors, it would take *Voyager 1* roughly 70,000 years to make the 4.3-light-year journey across interstellar space.

Super speeds

The universe has a rather inconvenient law we all must obey. Nothing can go faster than 983,571,056 feet (299,792,458 meters) per second—the maximum speed of a massless particle in a vacuum. Anything with mass, like the particles making up the atoms in your body, won't get anywhere close to that speed.

To cover the vast distances of space in a relatively short period of time, any technology we build needs to accelerate pretty quickly. One way to accomplish this is to use what's known as a slingshot effect. This involves aiming a space probe or vessel toward a planet or moon, where gravity gives the object an extra-hard tug. With a boost of speed, the space-bound technology will zip past the orbiting body and continue its journey faster than ever.

In 2016, NASA's *Juno* probe broke space speed records with a velocity of 165,000 miles (265,000 kilometers) per hour, thanks to a little help from Jupiter's gravity. That speed will be nothing compared with what the *Parker Solar Probe* could achieve as it dips toward the Sun in 2024. Its orbit could see it hit speeds of 430,000 miles (700,000 kilometers) per hour as it comes within a tiny 3.7 million miles (6 million kilometers) of the Sun's surface. If we want to leave our solar system, we're going to need something better than slingshots around stars or planets. NASA has been looking at different kinds of engines that can nudge an object to ever faster speeds.

The little engine that couldn't

Pushing technology through space relies on creating some kind of thrust, whether a puff of gas from a canister or charged particles zipping out of an ion drive. If it worked, a controversial propulsion system called a radio frequency resonant cavity thruster—or "EM drive"—could have slowly accelerated a small probe toward the speed of light using the thrust of radio waves. While it would never have enough energy to reach that limit, it would, in theory, beat the speed of any other thrust-based engine.

The engine itself is a metallic cone with electronic components that generate an electromagnetic field from a current. This field is channeled by the surrounding structure to create thrust. Prototypes have been created and even tested by engineers at NASA, who concluded such a device could produce a force just under one-thousandth of a newton.

That isn't very much. The downward push of an apple being held in your hand is about one newton. Yet it was a surprising result, and one that hinted at a new technology that could slowly push small objects to great speeds. There's just one problem; the laws of physics as we know them currently say this strange invention is impossible. Newton's third law says for there to be thrust, there must be an opposite action. If that happens in this engine, it's not clear how.

It's possible the thrust measured was caused by something else, like an effect of the planet's magnetic field. Or a problem with measurements. Maybe it does work after all! It's a problem future engineers will no doubt continue to debate.

Elevator to the sky

Getting off the surface of a planet is hard work. Gravity doesn't make it easy, and any fuel you need to blast off into space only makes a rocket heavier. It's a wonder we can leave at all.

In 1895, a Russian rocket scientist named Konstantin Tsiolkovsky was looking at the recently built Eiffel Tower and wondered if it was possible to build something so tall it could take people and cargo beyond the atmosphere into orbit.

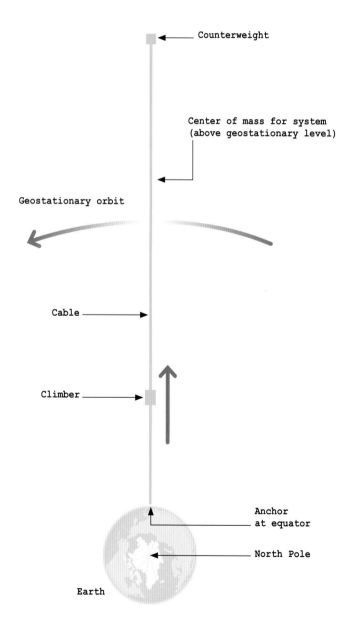

Counterweight

Center of mass for system
(above geostationary level)

Geostationary orbit

Cable

Climber

Anchor
at equator

North Pole

Earth

Since then, science-fiction authors and scientists have imagined ways of "climbing," rather than exploding, into space. On one hand, once built, a "space elevator" would carry objects sky-high at a much cheaper cost than rockets manage today.

The technology would rely on centrifugal force produced by our planet's rotation to hold up a long tether that's anchored near the equator, with a counterweight at the other end. With most of the mass beyond what's called a geostationary orbit (roughly 22,369 miles/36,000 kilometers above the surface), the cable would be pulled up from the planet, unlike a tower, which would be forced down by gravity.

Unfortunately, there are still no materials that could reliably handle the forces in such a huge structure. Until we find something strong enough, space elevators on Earth will remain science fiction.

PARKER SOLAR PROBE

NASA's *Parker Solar Probe* is the first mission intended to "touch" the Sun, to help astronomers understand why the outer layer, called a corona, is hotter than deeper layers. At its closest, the probe will be just over 3.7 million miles (6 million kilometers) from the Sun's surface. Engineers provided the probe with a special heat shield made of carbon to protect it against temperatures of more than 2,372°F (1,300°C), keeping its circuits a relatively cool 86°F (30°C).

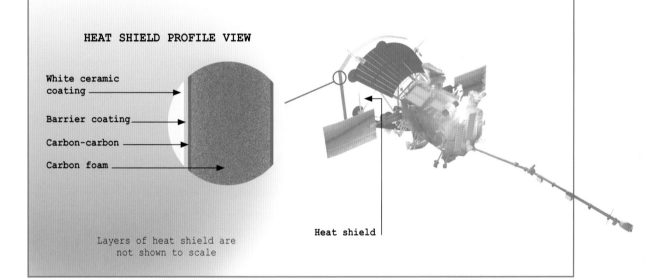

HEAT SHIELD PROFILE VIEW

White ceramic coating

Barrier coating

Carbon-carbon

Carbon foam

Layers of heat shield are not shown to scale

Heat shield

ANSWER THIS

1. What is the maximum speed anything can travel in the universe?

2. NASA's *Parker Solar Probe* could break speed records. How fast is it expected to travel around the Sun?

3. What is the problem with the theoretical EM drive?

4. What inspired Russian rocket scientist Konstantin Tsiolkovsky to imagine a tower we could climb into space?

5. If *Voyager 1* was aimed at the nearest star to Earth, how long would it take to get there at its current speed?

ASTEROID ENGINEERING

Floating about in the vast gap between Mars and Jupiter are countless chunks of minerals left over from the creation of the solar system. It's impossible to know exactly how many are in orbit. If you're only counting those that are over 330 feet (100 meters) across, there are at least 150 million of them.

Asteroids come in three types. About 75 percent are chondrites, or C-types. Those are made of a claylike material, with a sprinkling of silicates. Just under 20 percent are stony, or S-type asteroids, which are silicates and a mix of nickel and iron. The last few are metallic M-types, rich in nickel and iron, with a few other metals thrown in. These asteroids aren't common, but added together they would contain a huge reserve of metal resources. One of the biggest—a 140-mile (225-kilometer) wide asteroid called Psyche—could contain an untold fortune in iron and nickel.

As we rapidly use up resources here on Earth, sending landers out to mine asteroids is starting to look appealing. Engineers would need to build orbiting stations to support mining operations. Robotic landers would settle on a sizable M-type asteroid and work to dig up ore and then process it, sending the product back to orbiting stations. Even the fuel for transportation could be generated from raw materials on the asteroid.

Cataclysmic collisions

Asteroid discovery programs like NASA's Near-Earth Search Program have been keeping a close eye on the skies for decades, watching out for potentially hazardous chunks of space rock that would cause serious damage if it got too close. So far, there are just under 2,000 of these objects being monitored. What might we do if such a killer asteroid was found?

Engineers have a few ideas, including sending probes to steer the asteroid off course. Planting a nuclear bomb might work if it created a plume of gases that steered the asteroid in a new direction . . . or it might break one big rock into a whole number of smaller ones.

LIFE INSIDE A SPACE ROCK

Austrian architect and engineer Werner Grandl researches innovative ways we could colonize space. One of his ideas is to make asteroids habitable. An asteroid's surface is airless and bathed in radiation, but its core could be cleverly adapted.

Engineers would need to hollow out a large chamber inside the rock and seal it off. A nearby floating mirror could direct sunlight in through a window. Spinning the asteroid to create the right amount of centrifugal force could produce a gravity-like effect, just like home.

Incoming sunlight

Parabolic mirror array

Asteroid shell

Space to grow food

Living area

Light distribution cone

Elevator

Windows

Spaceport

ANSWER THIS

1. How many asteroids greater than 330 feet (100 meters) are there estimated to be between Mars and Jupiter?

2. What are the three types of asteroids?

3. What is special about the asteroid Psyche?

10.3 GOING SMALLER

What's the smallest thing you can see? If you've got excellent eyesight, you might see objects just one-tenth of a millimeter across. The world of nanotechnology involves engineering materials that are made from particles less than 100 nanometers in size—that's one ten-thousandth of a millimeter.

These are bigger than single atoms, but still small enough to have a unique set of characteristics. Take something as simple as gold, for example. Large pieces of this precious metal are a familiar pale yellow color. Pieces that are just tens of nanometers across mixed in a solution will reflect light in different ways, making them look reddish, or even purple.

Nanotechnology has been around for a while, but engineers are learning more about the properties of different materials as they shrink down. Sometimes this increases their surface area, exposing more of a material to their surroundings. Sometimes it changes how they stick together, or how they absorb radiation. Here are a number of ways tiny tech will become big news in the future.

Structures that heal themselves
Microscopic cracks in metal can quickly become catastrophic failures over time. The way some materials behave on a small scale could be used to help structures fix any small fractures that appear, by forming new bonds under certain kinds of light, or leaking into cracks and gluing them shut.

Sending medications to the right spot
Whenever you take medication, the drug spreads everywhere into most of your body's tissues. This is a waste if it's only intended for one spot, and can risk causing side effects. Having a nano-sized drug delivery service for your body would help keep medicines on target. Engineers are working on tiny capsules that can be guided through the body, releasing their contents on cue in just the right spot.

Keeping things clean

Keeping dust and water from surfaces can be hard work, but in some areas—such as aviation—an icy, dirty surface can be deadly. Nanomaterials with special textures that repel other substances are already leading to coatings that can keep surfaces dry. Special "oleophobic" materials repel grease and oil; just the thing for making engine parts super-slippery. Nanoparticles have also been developed to destroy potentially dangerous bacteria. As many deadly species become resistant to antibiotics, new ways to combat infection will be needed. Nanotechnology will play a bigger role in making materials that can keep bacteria at bay far more easily.

ANSWER THIS

1. How big are nanoparticles?

2. What color is a solution of gold nanoparticles?

3. How might nanotechnology be useful in medicine?

4. What are "oleophobic" materials?

MADE SIMPLE
CARBON NANOMATERIALS

Carbon is perfectly suited to nanoengineering as an element that can take a variety of forms. Carbon "quantum" dots are nanoparticles with protective coatings.

CARBON DOTS

FULLERENE

CARBON NANOTUBE

GRAPHENE

Graphene sheets have amazing electrical and structural properties, and can be rolled into nanotubes and other robust structures.

10.4 BUILDING NEW WORLDS

Some items that are designed and produced by engineers are safety-critical: if they should fail or malfunction, they could cause serious injury—or even death. Designs that are safety-critical must be engineered very carefully, and actions put in place to avoid a disaster if something should fail. Such products could be part of an aircraft or medical equipment. But what about on larger scales? How about entire worlds?

Engineering has the potential to turn inhospitable planets into new homes by changing the atmosphere, adding energy, or reshaping the geology. It's even possible to create a world from scratch, if you think big enough. The sky isn't the limit with engineering.

FACT

Billions of years ago, as our planet grew from similar chunks of rock and dust, most of its heavy metals sank toward its core, leaving the rocks of our crust light on precious minerals. Asteroids raining down on the surface might have provided the relatively small amounts of iron and nickel we find today.

Redesigning Mars

If you were to take the harshest places to live on Earth and combine them, it wouldn't come close to the extreme challenges a person would face on Mars. With an atmosphere thinner than the air on the tallest mountains, soil more toxic than the saltiest plains, and less water than the driest deserts, Mars isn't exactly paradise. Many of these harsh conditions could change with a future field of engineering called terraforming. It seems like an impossible task, until we remember Earth's own conditions have changed a lot in the past. In just two centuries, humans have affected the global climate simply by adding large amounts of carbon dioxide to the atmosphere.

Changing the conditions on Mars to suit human habitation would involve three things: thickening the atmosphere, adding heat, and protecting the surface from damaging levels of radiation. None of these tasks would be easy, and would require technology we haven't yet invented. Here are several possible ways they could be achieved.

Darkening the planet

Thanks to being farther from the Sun, Mars receives less than two-thirds of the sunlight that reaches Earth. It doesn't help that a lot of that light reflects back into space thanks to what's referred to as its albedo. Mars is one of the darkest planets in the solar system, turning about 70 percent of that sunlight into heat, but its patches of white ice and bright orange rock and dust covering the planet still bounce rays of light into space rather easily.

It might be possible to generate a little more heat by darkening the planet farther and decreasing the albedo. Dull-colored dust from its moons might be spread across its caps, for example, melting the ice into carbon dioxide and perhaps even releasing liquid water.

To get more sunlight, engineers could devise massive shiny sails that unfold in orbit around Mars to act like space mirrors. If they are angled right, these "synthetic stars" might reflect a little more light onto the surface and warm it up a touch.

SMALL BEGINNINGS

Living off-world won't be easy to begin with. Protective shells would be needed to shield life from radiation and to provide warmth and an atmosphere. However, with time, an entire planet could be engineered to do these tasks.

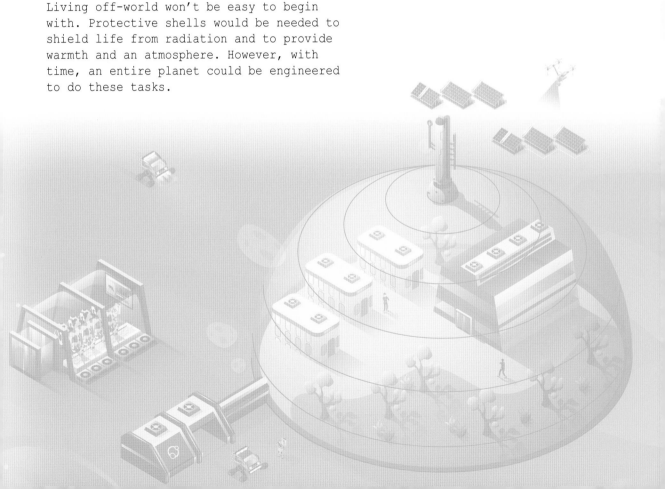

Importing gases

Unfortunately, no matter how much energy is added, the planet will still cool back down again in no time, losing that heat to space. The atmosphere on Earth has a pressure of about 100 kilopascals (kPa). If this were to drop below 6 kPa, the liquid on your skin and in your lungs would quickly boil away. On Mars, this pressure is just 1 kPa.

Adding gases would act like a blanket, help keep the planet warm, while also reducing the need for humans to wear heated pressure suits on the surface. One way to add gases like water vapor or carbon dioxide would be to redirect comets or asteroids toward the planet and "skim" them through the Martian atmosphere. Warming the planet's ice caps could also release these gases. A thicker atmosphere would in turn trap more heat by creating a greenhouse effect like the one on Earth. Other additives, like chlorofluorocarbons, are pollutants here, but sending rockets full of these chemicals to Mars could slowly create an atmospheric blanket that warms the frozen surface.

FACT

Technology that could be used to terraform other planets might help rewind the impact excess greenhouse gases have had on Earth. Adding reflective particles to the atmosphere, or helping organisms absorb carbon dioxide in the oceans, might help cool the planet again. Some think the risk of this kind of geoengineering is too big. If we get it wrong, we only have one planet to call home.

Turning red into green

Life has had a remarkable ability to transform our planet's chemistry, and could also do the same on Mars. By selecting the right organisms to withstand the extreme conditions on the planet, or even genetically create specialized life, it might be possible to release oxygen to thicken the atmosphere and break down toxins in the environment. They'd even darken rocks, decreasing the surface's albedo.

Just as ecosystems evolve in stages here, new organisms could be added over time to continue the process. Bacteria, algae, and fungi could eventually make some places on Mars safe enough for plants, and even some hardy animals.

DYSON SPHERE

Redesigning planets to make them habitable has nothing on one of the biggest engineering ideas ever, called a Dyson Sphere. Named after physicist Freeman Dyson, who discussed the concept in a 1960 science paper, the megastructure is a shell of orbiting solar cells that capture a large percentage of a star's light and convert it to other forms of energy for a civilization to use.

If alien engineers have made such technology, it might look like a lot of infrared heat coming from a place where we'd expect to see more starlight.

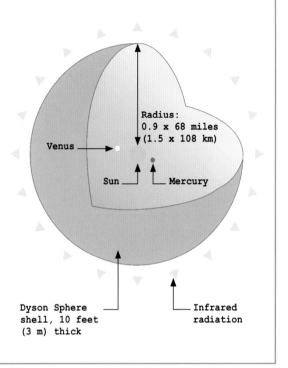

Radius:
0.9 x 68 miles
(1.5 x 108 km)

Venus

Sun · Mercury

Dyson Sphere shell, 10 feet (3 m) thick

Infrared radiation

Just because we can . . .

Terraforming Mars might one day be possible. But just because we can, doesn't mean we should. Many argue that Mars—indeed, all planets—should be left in a pristine state. Even if there is no life currently on Mars, changing it so drastically could make it harder to study its geological history. What's your opinion?

ANSWER THIS

1. What three problems would terraforming Mars need to solve?

2. What is the "albedo" of a planet?

3. What would the air pressure on Mars do to the liquid on your skin?

4. How might adding gases to the Martian atmosphere keep it warm?

5. What is a Dyson Sphere?

IMPOSSIBLE ENGINEERING?

With skyscrapers that push through the clouds, computers we can hold in our pockets, and space vessels that orbit the planet, it sometimes seems like we've built the impossible. Yet while some future endeavors will be challenging, others—for now—are likely to be impossible, thanks to what we currently know about the laws of physics.

In 2009, the famous physicist Stephen Hawking threw a party. Nobody showed up. The fact he sent the invitations out after it had finished might explain it, but in Hawking's defense, time travelers from the future should have gone back to make an appearance. It was a funny way to show that traveling back in time might always be impossible. Hawking also knew that physics makes reverse time travel rather unlikely, no matter how advanced engineering becomes in the future.

Albert Einstein's theory of general relativity does say some sorts of time-bending exist. His model says time and space doesn't have the same measurement everywhere. It all depends on things like gravity and changes in speed. If you zoom away from home at close to the speed of light, and zoom back again after a year, those at home would have been waiting for your return for a lot longer than a year. Traveling quickly could be like time traveling into the future: the closer you get to light speed, the slower your time seems to get compared with the time back home.

Faster than light?

If you went as fast as a photon of light, an instant of your time might seem like an eternity for the universe. However, physicists learned more than a century ago that information can't be sent faster than light speed. Worse still, this speed is slowed down when it gains mass. To make it go faster, you need to add energy. According to the law $E = mc^2$, adding energy adds mass, which requires even more energy to be accelerated, which adds even more mass . . . and so on! There's not energy in the universe that can push even a tiny spaceship fast enough. Although, some physicists wonder if we can use general relativity to bend space to make light-speed travel possible . . .

FREE ENERGY MACHINES

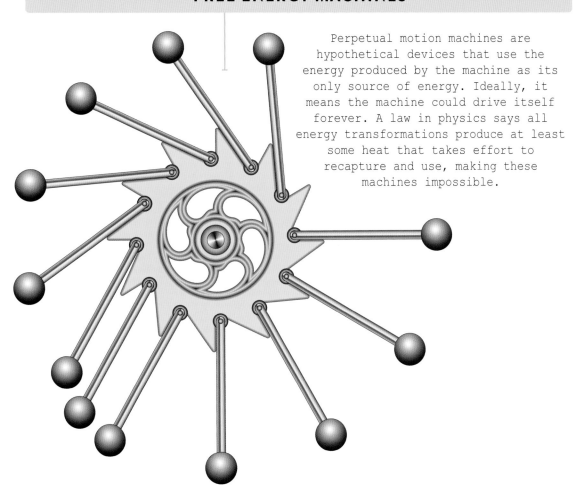

Perpetual motion machines are hypothetical devices that use the energy produced by the machine as its only source of energy. Ideally, it means the machine could drive itself forever. A law in physics says all energy transformations produce at least some heat that takes effort to recapture and use, making these machines impossible.

ANSWER THIS

1. Why didn't anybody come to Stephen Hawking's party in 2009?

2. If you leave Earth close to the speed of light and return a year later, how much time would have passed back home: one year, less than a year, or more than a year?

3. To make a mass move faster, you need to provide it with energy. According to the law $E = mc^2$, what happens to this energy?

4. Why can't the energy from a machine be used to keep it running forever?

FUTURE ENGINEERING

1. **How long would it take light to cross from one side of the Milky Way to the other?**

   a. About 100,000 years

   b. About 1,000 years

   c. About 100 years

   d. No time at all; light moves instantaneously

2. **How does the slingshot effect accelerate spacecraft?**

   a. A giant rubber band shoots the spacecraft into space

   b. The spacecraft "falls" toward a moon or planet in orbit, which pulls it into a faster speed

   c. The spacecraft catches sunlight on a giant sail

   d. There's no such thing as a slingshot effect

3. **What would keep a theoretical space elevator from falling down?**

   a. The inertia of centrifugal force

   b. Very strong carbon fibers

   c. Flying buttresses

   d. Rockets

4. **What is the *Parker Solar Probe*'s mission?**

   a. To touch down on the Sun's surface

   b. To fly into the middle of the Sun

   c. To capture images of the dark side of the Sun

   d. To directly measure the Sun's corona

5. **What is a C-type asteroid?**

   a. Asteroid made of chalk

   b. Comet

   c. Asteroid made from claylike materials and silicates

   d. Piece of another planet or moon

   Answers on page 218

6. **Where might the heavy metals of Earth's crust have come from?**

   a. Collision from another planet

   b. Bombardment of asteroids

   c. Radiation from the Sun

   d. Comets from another solar system

7. **What is nanotechnology?**

   a. The engineering of materials made of particles less than 1 nanometer in size

   b. The engineering of materials made of particles more than 100 nanometers in size

   c. The engineering of materials made of particles less than 100 nanometers in size

   d. The engineering of materials made of particles invisible to the naked eye

SIMPLE SUMMARY

As we learn more about how the universe works, technology will continue to overcome challenges to make stronger materials, more powerful machines, and faster electronics.

- The universe has a rather inconvenient law we all must obey. Nothing can go faster than 983,571,056 feet (299,792,458 meters) per second—the maximum speed of a massless particle in a vacuum.

- NASA's *Parker Solar Probe* is the first mission intended to "touch" the Sun, to help astronomers understand why the outer layer, called a corona, is hotter than deeper layers.

- Floating about in the vast gap between Mars and Jupiter are countless chunks of minerals left over from the creation of the solar system. Asteroids come in three types: chondrites, or C-types; stony, or S-types; and M-types.

- The world of nanotechnology involves engineering materials that are made from particles less than 100 nanometers in size—that's one ten-thousandth of a millimeter.

- Challenges a person would face on Mars include an atmosphere thinner than the air on the tallest mountains, soil more toxic than the saltiest plains, and less water than the driest deserts.

- Terraforming could change the conditions on Mars to suit human habitation, which would involve thickening the atmosphere, adding heat, and protecting the surface from damaging levels of radiation.

- While some future endeavors will be challenging, others—for now—are likely to be impossible, thanks to what we currently know about the laws of physics.

TECHNOLOGY TIMELINE

For over 95 percent of the time that our species has been on Earth, our most significant technological advances were stone tools, fire, and simple boats. The first major change in the way we lived came 12,000 years ago, when some humans in the Middle East began farming. As more people settled, they had a greater need for tools, possessions, and permanent shelters, and started to form larger communities.

WHAT YOU WILL LEARN

INFLUENTIAL INVENTIONS

Some inventions changed our lives more than others. These each led to huge changes in society by changing how we live and making many new technologies possible. They all continue to influence every aspect of our lives today.

Wheels

Pottery wheels first appeared in the Middle East around 5200 BC. After about 1,500 years, someone had the bright idea to put them on plows, making them easier to drag along, and most vehicles still use them. Wheels aren't just useful for getting around, though; waterwheels, flywheels, pulleys, cogs, and record players use them too.

Steel furnaces

Most metal objects—from cars to cutlery—are made of steel, which is iron that has some carbon mixed in to strengthen it. Being cheaper and stronger than bronze, it became the metal of choice after the first furnaces appeared in Turkey in 1800 BC. We still churn out 1.4 billion tons of it a year, and use it extensively in construction.

Guns

Guns are responsible for many of the worst aspects of history but have had a massive influence on who we are as a species. Invented in China in the 13th century, they shifted the balance of power from those with the biggest, strongest armies to those who could kill from a distance, allowing a few nations to colonize vast areas of the globe and causing many of the inequalities and conflicts found across the world today.

The printing press

The ability to reproduce text cheaply and quickly had a huge impact on the pace of technological advancement. Its invention in 1439 allowed old and new ideas to spread easily and, since the early 1600s, the pace of change has been immense. Even though we now rely more on screens for reading, books and newspapers are still all around us.

Microscopes

By making cells and microbes visible, microscopes have allowed us to understand the cause of many diseases. The resulting medical advances that resulted from this have led to average life spans doubling in the last hundred years.

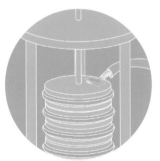

Voltaic piles

Batteries have changed a lot since 1800 but have never stopped being useful. As the first reliable way to generate an electric current, voltaic piles allowed the experimentation that led to the early electrical inventions. As batteries improve, they will help us to rid ourselves of fossil fuels by powering vehicles and storing energy from wind and solar power.

Photography

Developed in the 1830s, photography was the first invention to accurately record what we see so that we can look at it later. For most of the time since, photography has been for professionals and hobbyists, but the smartphone means that most people carry cameras everywhere they go, and they are a routine way for us to communicate online.

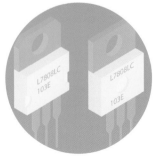

Transistors

Inside a smartphone, there are around 500 billion transistors. In fact, there are transistors in almost every piece of electrical equipment on Earth, and in the 70 years since they were invented, they have become the most manufactured item in history.

TIMELINE: 10,000 BC TO AD 1500

Twelve thousand years ago, our ancestors began farming for the first time. Nomadic tribes settled and formed communities. Being permanently settled led to the first buildings and created the need for specialist farming tools and the best weapons to protect our property.

For most of this period, change was very slow. However, 5,000 years ago, as the Bronze Age started, writing and mathematics developed, allowing communities to become larger and more organized. Wheels allowed farmers to be more productive and freed up time for people to have specialized jobs, which enabled more advances in building and machinery.

By the end of this period, a number of civilizations had contributed to technological advances. There were roads connecting Europe and Asia, and the American continent had been discovered by Europeans. We had gone from living in small tribes to living in a global community.

■ Science and math

■ Building

■ Power

■ Machines

■ Transport

■ Chemical

■ Medical

■ Communications

1. First bricks in Syria 9500 BC

2. Age of Göbekli Tepe in Turkey 9000 BC

3. First use of copper 8000 BC

4. Earliest known smelting of lead 6500 BC

5. Earliest known wheels found in Middle East 5200 BC

6. Earliest known smelting of copper in Serbia 5000 BC

7. First sewing needles 4400 BC

8. Log roads built in England and paved streets in the Middle East 4000 BC

9. First wheeled vehicles in Iraq 3700 BC

10. Writing invented in Iraq 3400 BC

1

2

3

4

5

6

7

10,000 BC

7500 BC

5000 BC

11. First sailing boats in Egypt 3200 BC

12. Earliest known use of arithmetic and geometry 3000 BC

13. First bronze made with copper and tin 3000 BC

14. Egyptian texts describe electricity in eels 2750 BC

15. Building of Great Pyramid 2560 BC

16. Papyrus (early paper) developed in Egypt 2500 BC

17. First paved road in Egypt 2200 BC

18. Earliest glass in Egypt 1600 BC

19. Stonehenge 2000 BC

20. Earliest known steel 1800 BC

21. Rubber used in Mesoamerica 1600 BC

22. First iron smelted 1200 BC

23. Earliest known prosthetic 950 BC

24. Thales of Miletus writes about static electricity 600 BC

25. First crane in Greece 515 BC

26. Pythagoras 570–495 BC

27. First waterwheels 400 BC

28. Roman roads built across Europe from 312 BC

29. Chinese invent early magnetic compass 300 BC

30. Archimedes 287–212 BC

31. Antikythera mechanism 100 BC

32. First rudders on boats in China 1st century AD

33. First arch bridge 300

34. Romans invent early concrete 300

35. First oil wells in China 347

36. First tar roads in Persia 850

37. First gunpowder in China 800

38. Flying buttresses become common in architecture 1100

39. Chinese invent rockets and guns 1200s

40. First glasses in Italy 1286

41. Mādhava's first accurate calculation of pi 1400

42. Printing press 1439

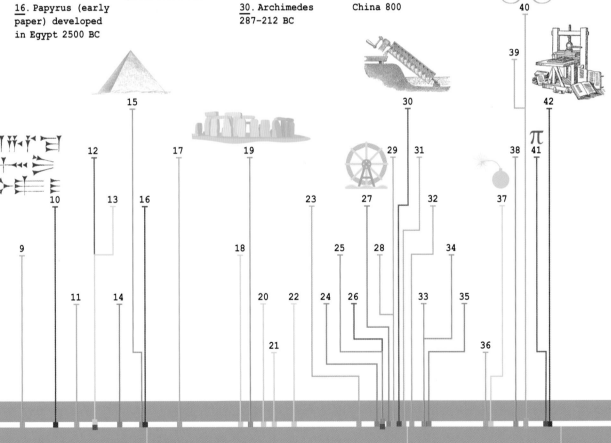

2500 BC

0

1500

TIMELINE:
1500–1900

Over the next four centuries, international trade became common and scientific discoveries opened the possibilities of new inventions. Our new understanding of physics and chemistry allowed us to invent thousands of devices to make our lives more convenient. Engines took away the work that had previously been done by animals, and by the end of the 19th century, trains and steamships had made long-distance travel comfortable and fast. Electrical devices also developed throughout the 19th century so that by the turn of the 20th century, the world had become modern, with radios, telephones, fridges, and electric lights available to the public.

Science
and math

Building

Power

Machines

Transport

Chemical

Medical

Communications

1. First circumnavigation of the globe 1521

2. Early compound microscopes 1600

3. Galileo improves telescope design 1609

4. Drebbel builds first submarine 1620

5. Pascal invents a mechanical calculator 1642

6. Von Guericke invents a vacuum pump 1650

7. Huygen's pendulum clock 1656

8. Isaac Newton describes forces 1687

9. Gottfried Leibniz develops binary code 1687

10. Fahrenheit invents the thermometer 1709

11. First commercial steam engine 1711

12. First accurate sea clock invented by John Harrison 1736

13. Bernoulli effect first described 1738

14. Benjamin Franklin invents the lightning rod 1752

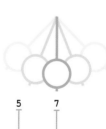

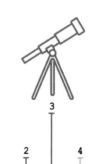

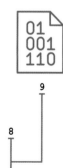

1

2

3

4

5

6

7

8

9

1500

1600

15. First steam-powered passenger vehicle 1769

16. Montgolfier brothers' hot-air balloon 1783

17. Electrolysis developed, which allows discovery of many new elements 1785

18. Jenner develops the first vaccine 1798

19. Alessandro Volta invents the voltaic pile 1800

20. Jacquard weaving loom is the first programmable machine 1801

21. John Dalton develops modern atomic theory 1802

22. First steam locomotive 1802

23. First blood transfusion 1812

24. Brunel invents tunneling shield 1818

25. First practical electric motor 1834

26. Photography first developed 1830s

27. Morse code invented 1837

28. James Joule demonstrates conservation of energy 1840

29. First safety elevator 1852

30. First controlled flight in a dirigible 1852

31. Aspirin first synthesized 1853

32. First commercial refrigerator 1856

33. First transatlantic telegraph 1858

34. First rechargeable battery 1859

35. First underground railway in London 1863

36. Nobel invents dynamite 1867

37. First telephone 1876

38. Modern internal combustion engine 1876

39. Phonograph records and plays back sounds 1877

40. Invention of the light bulb 1879

41. First public electricity supply in U.S. 1882

42. J.K. Starley's Rover bicycle 1885

43. Radio waves discovered 1886

44. First radio broadcast 1895

45. First film 1895

46. Discovery of X-rays 1895

47. J. J. Thompson discovers electrons 1897

1700

1800

1900

TIMELINE: 1900-2000

The beginning of the 20th century saw the development of electrical and mechanical machines, making it faster and cheaper to communicate. As a result of scientific activity during World War II, nuclear power and computers became possible and the advances in rocket technology led to humans going to space for the first time. Genetic discoveries meant that biology could be engineered, and by the end of the century the first cloned mammal had been born. Passenger air travel, satellites, and consumer electronics meant that anyone could talk to anyone else on the planet instantly, or travel there in hours.

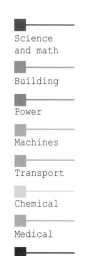

Science and math

Building

Power

Machines

Transport

Chemical

Medical

Communications

1. First vacuum cleaner 1901

2. Wright brothers' first airplane 1903

3. Bakelite is the first commonly used plastic 1907

4. Model T Ford is the first affordable car 1908

5. Salvarsan is the first "magic bullet" 1909

6. Haber process fixes nitrogen for fertilizer 1909

7. Rutherford discovers atomic nucleus 1911

8. First use of the word "robot" 1920

9. First televisions 1920s

10. Nuclear fission discovered by Lise Meitner and Otto Hahn 1938

11. First jet airplane 1939

12. First practical helicopter 1939

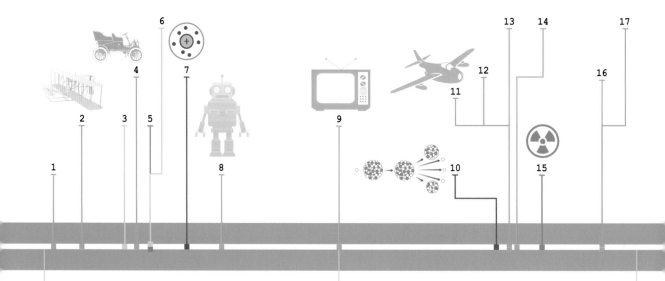

1900

1925

1950

13. Defibrillator invented 1939

14. First ultrasound image 1940

15. First nuclear reactor 1942

16. First transistor 1947

17. First jet plane to break the sound barrier 1947

18. First atomic clock 1955

19. First hard disk 1956

20. *Sputnik* is the first satellite 1957

21. First lasers 1958

22. *Vanguard I* satellite is the first machine powered by solar panels 1958

23. First silicon chip 1959

24. First pacemaker 1960

25. First human in space, Yuri Gagarin 1961

26. First LEDs 1962

27. First fiber-optic data transmission 1965

28. First networked computer 1969

29. First human on the Moon, Neil Armstrong 1969

30. First pocket calculator 1970

31. First home computer 1976

32. First IVF baby 1978

33. First maglev train in Germany 1979

34. First cell phone 1984

35. First lithium batteries 1985

36. World Wide Web is the first web browser 1990

37. First 3-D printer 1992

38. Channel Tunnel opens 1994

39. Dolly the sheep is the first cloned animal 1995

40. First DVD 1995

41. Thrust SSC, only land vehicle to break the sound barrier 1997

42. First social media web platforms 1997

43. First smartphones in Japan 1999

20
21
22
29
19
28
18
23 25 26
30
32
34 36
38 40
42
41
35
37
24
27
31 33
43
39

WWW

1975

2000

TIMELINE: THE TWENTY-FIRST CENTURY

The achievements of the first 20 years of the 21st century demonstrate how all of the technologies and discoveries of the past can come together into single machines and structures. There are new discoveries every day, but only time will tell if they are to be as influential as the inventions that made the modern world.

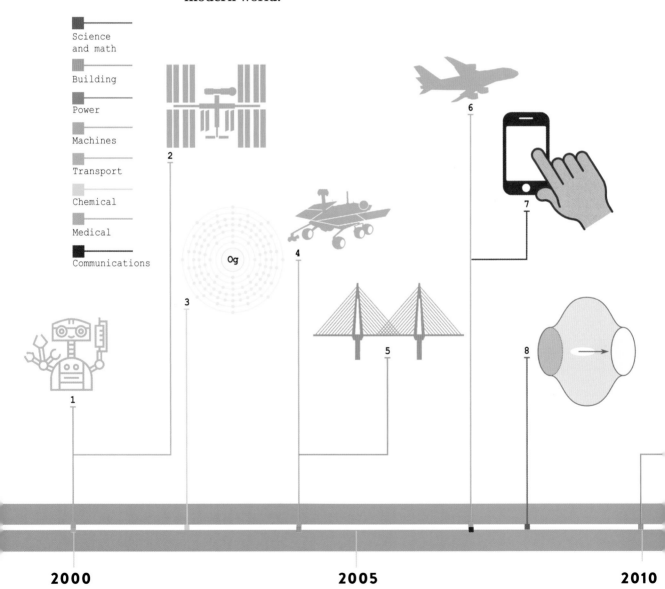

Science and math

Building

Power

Machines

Transport

Chemical

Medical

Communications

2000

2005

2010

1. First robotic surgeon 2000

2. First residents arrive at the International Space Station 2000

3. Oganesson, element 118, first created 2002

4. Opportunity lands on Mars 2004

5. Millau Viaduct, world's tallest bridge 2004

6. Airbus A380, the world's largest jet, goes into service 2007

7. The iPhone is the first phone to use a large touchscreen for interacting 2007

8. Large Hadron Collider becomes operational 2008

9. Burj Khalifa, world's tallest building 2010

10. Vantablack is the darkest paint ever created 2014

11. Three Gorges Dam in China becomes world's largest power station 2015

12. First three-parent baby born 2016

13. First genetically modified baby 2018

14. Over 50 percent of the world's population use the Internet 2018

15. First commercial quantum computer 2019

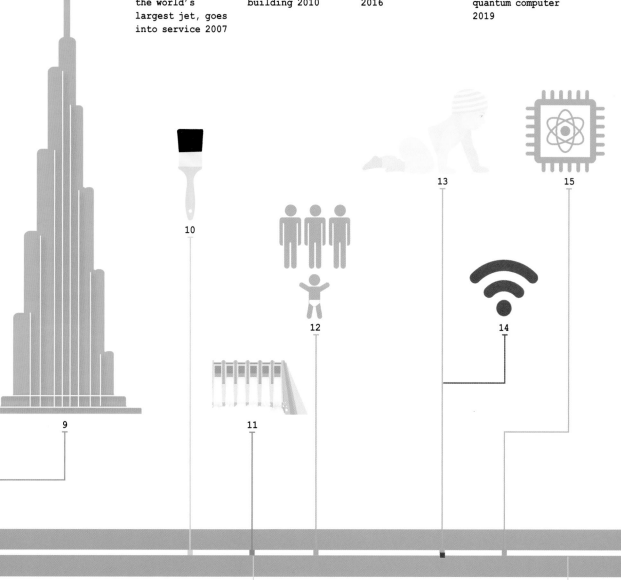

2015

2020

NOTES

SIMPLE SUMMARY

The first major change in the way we lived came 12,000 years ago, when some humans in the Middle East began farming. As more people settled, they had a greater need for tools, possessions, and permanent shelters, and started to form larger communities.

• Some inventions changed our lives more than others, leading to huge changes in society by changing how we live and making many new technologies possible.

• Twelve thousand years ago, our ancestors began farming for the first time. Nomadic tribes settled and formed communities.

• Five thousand years ago, as the Bronze Age started, writing and mathematics developed, allowing communities to become larger and more organized.

• Wheels allowed farmers to be more productive and freed up time for people to have specialized jobs, which enabled more advances in building and machinery.

• Electrical devices developed throughout the 19th century so that by the turn of the 20th century, the world had become modern, with radios, telephones, fridges, and electric lights available to the public.

• The beginning of the 20th century saw the development of electrical and mechanical machines, such as radios, telephones, and cars, making it faster and cheaper to communicate.

• The achievements of the first 20 years of the 21st century demonstrate how all of the technologies and discoveries of the past can come together into single machines and structures.

ANSWERS

LESSON 1: WHAT IS ENGINEERING?

ANSWER THIS

1.2 Skill Set

1. Employability skills
2. -
3. Science, technology, engineering, and math
4. Team, mix
5. The ability to work in a team, use initiative and be self-motivated, work to deadlines, communicate, understand numeracy/IT, problem solve, and organize

1.3 Economics of Engineering

1. Cost saving
2. International Space Station
3. $42 billion
4. Is it safe, how much will the materials cost, how much will it cost to build, how long will it take to build, etc.

1.5 Who Are Engineers?

1. False: It is increasing and increasing, faster and faster all the time!
2. False: The best designs are aerodynamic and look sleek and beautiful
3. Civil, chemical, mechanical, process, robotics, software, electrical, aerospace, nuclear, computer hardware, energy, agricultural, automotive, environmental
4. A mix of a team of engineers including: robotics engineer, mechanical engineer, electrical engineer, and software engineer
5. Roads, buildings, airports, hospitals—anything to do with buildings, towns, and cities

QUIZ TIME

1. c
2. c
3. b
4. a
5. c
6. b
7. d

LESSON 2: SCIENCE OF ENGINEERING

ANSWER THIS

2.1 From Science to Technology

1. To test understanding of nature
2. Ibn al-Haytham
3. The most stable structures are wider at the bottom than at the top
4. The Burj Khalifa in Dubai
5. To test the strength and stability of the rocks and ground underneath

2.3 Engineering for Science

1. To find new subatomic particles
2. Because neutrinos are very unlikely to interact with matter
3. To find planets in other solar systems
4. Gravitational waves

2.4 Pushing and Pulling

1. A push or a pull
2. Because you would need to be in deep space, away from the Earth's gravity and atmosphere

3. Because it has less mass

4. When fuel explodes and turns to gas, it is pushed down by the rocket, which means the rocket is pushed up by the gas

2.5 Tiny Building Blocks

1. Chemical reactions

2. Protons, neutrons, and electrons

3. Negative

4. Outer electrons from one atom are attracted to the nucleus of another atom

5. Intermolecular bonds

2.6 Balance of Energy

1. The joule

2. It gains kinetic energy as it falls, which is stored as thermal energy at the bottom

3. Energy stored as movement

4. Gravitational, kinetic, elastic, thermal, magnetic, electrostatic, chemical, nuclear

5. Energy stored as movement

QUIZ TIME

1. c
2. a
3. b
4. b
5. a
6. c
7. d
8. d
9. b

LESSON 3: BUILDING STRUCTURES

ANSWER THIS

3.1 Ancient Construction

1. As a temple or ceremonial site

2. Development of harder metals like bronze and iron

3. Memorials and tombs for the dead

4. Around 40,000 years old

5. Sandstone

3.2 Sky's the Limit

1. Arches called flying buttresses

2. 2,723 feet (830 meters) tall

3. To get people to the top in elevators and to find ways to get people down safely in the event of a fire

4. Nearly 4,000 years

3.3 Building Bridges

1. A mechanical force that squeezes materials together

2. A mechanical force that pulls materials apart

3. Suspension bridge

4. Arched bridge

5. Because the timing of many people moving across the bridge caused a buildup of swinging motion

3.4 Digging Deep

1. Digging through hard, soft, or brittle materials; tunnels flooding with groundwater; hitting pockets of gas

2. A wall of iron scaffolding that protects workers as they dig a tunnel

3. 11

4. 1990

5. 7.5 miles (12.2 kilometers)

QUIZ TIME

1. b
2. c
3. a
4. d
5. a
6. c
7. d
8. a
9. d

LESSON 4: POWER AND ENGINEERING

ANSWER THIS

4.1 Energy Sources

1. An energy source that cannot be reused

2. Wood

3. Living things are buried and slowly change into fuels over millions of years as a result of heat and pressure

4. In Persia in the ninth century

5. Batteries, nuclear reactions, geothermal energy, and tidal energy

4.2 Electricity

1. Electrostatic forces caused by the charge on protons and electrons
2. An early battery made from copper and zinc disks, separated by paper soaked in saltwater
3. Electrons
4. It is when charge flows backward and forward, rather than continuously in the same direction
5. They are clear and easy to read

4.3 Generating Electricity

1. Michael Faraday
2. Magnets in a generator interact with the magnetic field created by moving a wire to push electrons through the wire
3. With more coils of wire, being turned faster, and a stronger magnet
4. It is two or more cells joined together
5. When current is created by a material changing shape

4.4 Powering Nations

1. To boil water
2. They heat up
3. To increase the voltage and reduce the current for the distribution of electricity

4. To reduce the voltage and make it safe for use in the home
5. During the night

4.5 Going Green

1. Carbon dioxide
2. Acid rain and breathing problems
3. Energy can still be available when the wind does not blow or when the sun does not shine
4. A flywheel

QUIZ TIME

1. c
2. b
3. c
4. a
5. c
6. d
7. a
8. c
9. b
10. d

LESSON 5: TRANSPORT

ANSWER THIS

5.1 Getting Around

1. 6,000 years ago
2. Electricity could be supplied through the rails instead of being supplied by batteries
3. So that water would drain away
4. Tarmac

5.2 Personal Transport

1. Cars and bicycles

2. To absorb the impact of hitting small bumps
3. It is strong but very light
4. They have a streamlined shape
5. They produce noise and air pollution, and are dangerous for pedestrians and other road users

5.3 Public Transit

1. It is often cheaper and more efficient
2. 1826
3. The London Underground, built in 1863
4. They produce fewer emissions of greenhouse gases that contribute to climate change
5. Maglev trains have no moving parts, so there is no friction

5.4 Boats and Subs

1. Human-powered rowing, wind, burning fuels, batteries, or nuclear power
2. The upward force on a floating object will equal the weight of fluid pushed out of the way
3. As the rudder turns, the water resistance becomes greater on one side, giving the boat a sideways push
4. It allowed boats to sail into the wind by tacking
5. By pumping water in and out of air tanks

5.5 Taking Flight

1. The Montgolfier brothers' hot-air balloon in 1783
2. An object that feels force on one side more than another as it moves through a liquid or gas
3. Air resistance and the Bernoulli effect
4. They are fast and can land in busy or remote places

5.6 Space and Beyond

1. China in the 13th century
2. *Sputnik*, a Russian satellite
3. Leaving the atmosphere, reentering the atmosphere, the vacuum of space, a lack of gravity, cosmic radiation
4. Have a blunt shape, a surface covered in heatproof tiles, and a substance that crumbles off when it gets hot
5. To protect themselves from dangerous bursts of radiation

5.7 Future Transport

1. They have faster reactions than humans
2. No energy is wasted due to air resistance, allowing vehicles to travel much faster
3. Less ground space is needed for roads and parking

4. They can fly like airplanes at lower altitudes and do not have parts that are discarded

QUIZ TIME

1. d
2. a
3. a
4. b
5. c
6. d
7. c
8. b
9. a
10. d

LESSON 6: MACHINES AT WORK

ANSWER THIS

6.1 Simple Machines

1. Levers, wheels, inclined planes
2. A fulcrum
3. They spread effort out over a distance
4. The force required to make an object move a certain distance

6.2 Machines Under Power

1. Convert energy to produce motion, which makes work easier
2. Ones that turn expanding gases into a motion and ones that use interactions between electrical currents and magnetism
3. Horsepower is a unit of power

4. They became efficient enough to get more power and were easier to control
5. Pump water out of mines

6.3 Measuring Time

1. The escapement
2. Christiaan Huygens
3. Allows a machine to swap speed for force, force for speed, or change the direction of a rotation
4. A shipwreck containing an ancient mechanism
5. Keeping track of celestial movements

6.4 Robotics

1. Robots are machines that can carry out a task without human direction
2. Dangerous or boring, repetitive jobs, like building cars
3. Opportunity
4. 4 to 24 minutes
5. A 1920 play by Karel Čapek called *Rossum's Universal Robots*

6.5 Intelligent Machines

1. It could perform just about any algorithm another machine could do
2. It uses components that behave similar to human brain cells
3. Artificial intelligence
4. The easy problem (making a device that acts as conscious as us) and the hard problem (knowing it really is as conscious as us)
5. Transistor

6.6 Quantum Computing

1. A portion, or a "particle" of something
2. According to rules of probability
3. A bit; in quantum computing this is a qubit
4. A "yet to be determined" state before a particle's properties are measured
5. Solve complex problems that would take too long for a classical computer to work out

6.7 Cool Technology

1. Ice houses
2. Refrigeration
3. Jacob Perkins
4. By using crystals that absorb energy as they change shape

QUIZ TIME

1. b
2. b
3. d
4. c
5. b
6. c
7. d
8. a

LESSON 7: CHEMICAL ENGINEERING

ANSWER THIS

7.1 Alchemy—Magic or Engineering?

1. Most likely around 2,500 years ago in ancient Greece
2. Small indivisible units called atoma
3. Earth, fire, air, and water
4. Robert Boyle

7.2 Smelting Through the Ages

1. A useful metal or mineral mixed with other elements as a compound, usually in a rock form
2. Smelting
3. Gold
4. Bloomeries
5. The process of electrolysis separates aluminum and oxygen ions dissolved in a solution of molten cryolite

7.4 Problems with Plastics

1. Polymers
2. Oil
3. Mechanical and chemical recycling
4. They have additives that make them hard to be chemically recycled

7.5 Fertile Grounds

1. From fertilizer compounds from the soil
2. By using human and animal waste
3. Around 80 percent
4. By combining nitrogen with hydrogen with a catalyst and pressure
5. Explosives in weapon production

QUIZ TIME

1. a
2. d
3. c
4. d
5. b
6. d
7. b
8. a

LESSON 8: BIOENGINEERING

ANSWER THIS

8.1 Pharmaceutical Engineering

1. By eating specific plants, fungi, and even minerals from the soil
2. An early antibiotic that could kill the bacterium responsible for syphilis
3. Kill microbes (specifically bacteria) without destroying the tissue of its host
4. In natural ecosystems, or by using computers to model new chemicals
5. Around $1 trillion

8.2 I Heart Engineering

1. They don't start "stopped" hearts—they reset hearts that aren't pumping rhythmically
2. Waves of charged particles moving in and out of its muscle cells
3. Quivering, or pumping in an uncoordinated fashion

4. A device that could record the heart's rhythm

5. The first reliable pacemaker that was small enough to be worn

8.3 Getting Under Your Skin

1. A form of electromagnetic radiation—or light waves—called X-rays

2. Magnetic resonance imaging

3. They emit a burst of energy that help produce an image of different tissues

4. They are too high-pitched

5. To capture images of babies while they are still in the womb

8.4 The Body Builders

1. Prosthetics

2. A human toe

3. The tasks of the cardiac and respiratory systems

4. They allowed blood to clot quickly

8.5 How Does Your Organ Grow?

1. Because the immune system can attack and kill donated tissues

2. In theory, stem cells

3. An extracellular matrix

4. Roughly 140,000

5. About $270,000

8.6 A Baby in the Lab

1. Around 85 percent

2. In vitro fertilization, which works by fertilizing an egg taken from a mother outside of the body, and implanting the embryo in a mother's uterus

3. The mitochondria

4. The mother

5. Dolly was the first animal to be born as an artificially produced clone through somatic cell transfer

8.7 Engineering Genes

1. A sequence of codes that defines how a task is performed inside a living organism

2. The restriction of which crops or livestock reproduce

3. It can select specific characteristics in living things, to remove diseases from livestock or make crops more pest-resistant

4. To protect themselves from viral infections

5. It could increase the risk of cancer in living humans

8.8 An Engineer in the Kitchen

1. By drying, salting, and smoking

2. Draws out additional moisture and creates a hostile environment that prevents microbes from growing easily

3. It can remove oxygen from foods that could ruin their color

4. Europe

QUIZ TIME

1. b
2. a
3. c
4. d
5. b
6. c
7. b
8. c

LESSON 9: COMMUNICATIONS

ANSWER THIS

9.1 Communications Past

1. About 500,000 years ago

2. The printing press

3. 1840s

4. The letter "E"

9.2 Waves of Communication

1. The telephone

2. Liquid transmitter

3. A Morse code signal for the letter "S," using radio waves

9.3 Going Digital

1. A code made from ones and zeros

2. A continuously changing signal

3. The sound is chopped into very short segments and a binary value is given to its pitch and volume

4. Noise can be removed before it is amplified and they can be sent through fiber-optic cables
5. It uses up very little space

9.4 A World of Data

1. ARPANET
2. The World Wide Web
3. The Internet of Things
4. A computer that stores and processes web pages
5. They are cheap and can access the Internet in remote areas

QUIZ TIME

1. c
2. b
3. b
4. c
5. a
6. a
7. b
8. c
9. a
10. d

LESSON 10: FUTURE ENGINEERING

ANSWER THIS

10.1 Reaching for the Stars

1. The speed of light, at 983,571,056 feet (299,792,458 meters) per second

2. It is expected to hit speeds of 429,989 miles (692,000 kilometers) per hour
3. It produces thrust without projecting mass in an opposite direction, which goes against Newton's third law of motion
4. The Eiffel Tower
5. 70,000 years

10.2 Asteroid Engineering

1. More than 150 million
2. C-class (clay and silicates), S-class (silicates and metals), M-class (metals)
3. It is a large M-class asteroid containing a fortune in metals like iron and nickel
4. 2014

10.3 Going Smaller

1. Particles less than 100 nanometers in size
2. Red to purple
3. They can carry drugs to specific locations in the body
4. Materials that repel oils

10.4 Building New Worlds

1. How to thicken its atmosphere, warm the surface, and increase protection from damaging radiation
2. The ability of a surface to reflect light
3. The low air pressure would allow liquid to easily boil on the skin

4. Like the greenhouse effect on Earth, gases could help trap heat close to the surface
5. A hypothetical megastructure of engineering that could surround a star and absorb a larger percentage of its light for energy

10.5 Impossible Engineering?

1. He only invited people from the future with invitations he sent out after the party
2. More than a year
3. Energy applied to make an object move faster adds more mass, making it harder to accelerate
4. When energy is transformed, a proportion becomes heat that requires more energy to transform into work

QUIZ TIME

1. a
2. b
3. a
4. d
5. c
6. b
7. c

FURTHER READING

Ask an Astronaut:
My Guide to Life in Space
Tim Peake
Arrow Books, 2018

Astronaut-Aquanaut: How Space Science
and Sea Science Interact
Jennifer Swanson
National Geographic Kids, 2018

Awesome Engineering Activities
for Kids
Christina Schul
Rockridge Press, 2019

Cars, Trains, Ships, Planes: A Visual
Encyclopaedia of Every Vehicle
DK, 2015

Engineer Academy
Steve Martin & Nastia Sleptsova
Ivy Press, 2017

Flight
Zack Scott
Wildfire, 2019

Hands-on Science
Edited by Sarah Kellett, David Shaw
& Kath Kovac
CSIRO Publishing, 2016

How to Be a Coder
Kiki Prottsman
DK Children, 2019

How to Be an Engineer
Carol Vorderman
DK, 2018

How Technology Works
DK, 2019

How We Got to Now: Six Innovations
that Made the Modern World
Steven Johnson
Penguin Young Readers/Viking BFYR, 2015

Inventor Lab: Awesome Builds
for Smart Makers
DK, 2019

Maker Lab: 28 Super Cool Projects
Jack Challoner
DK Publishing, 2016

Robot: Meet the Machines of the Future
DK Children, 2018

Save the Crash-test Dummies
Jennifer Swanson
Peachtree Publishing, 2019

Thing Explainer
Randall Munroe
John Murray, 2015

30-Second Engineering
James Trevelyan
Ivy Press, 2019

The Way Things Work
David Macaulay
DK, 2016

GLOSSARY

Acceleration How quickly something changes its speed, normally measured in meters per second squared.

Artificial intelligence (AI) Software that carries out tasks in a way that reminds us of the talents of a humanlike brain.

Atomic number The number of protons in an atom, a feature that determines what kind of element the atom is.

Buttress Building structure that transfers the downward force of a wall to provide additional support. A flying buttress is a lightweight version that makes use of an arch connecting to a separate pillar.

CRISPR Form of genetic engineering technology based on virus-killing biochemistry in bacteria.

Defibrillator Medical device that applies a current across the heart to reset its natural pulsing rhythm.

Digital Information that is communicated using just two states, such as an electrical signal that is either on or off.

Drag The forces that slow an object down, which are usually friction and air resistance.

Efficient Not wasteful. Can be used to describe a process or machine that does not waste materials, energy, money, or time.

Electric current The flow of charged particles (normally the free electrons of the metal atoms in wires). The faster or bigger the flow, the more energy can be transferred by it.

Energy The ability of something to cause a change, such as a change in temperature or speed.

Escapement Simple device that transfers a force in a controlled way. In clocks, it turns the push of an unwinding spring or falling mass into something that can measure time.

Fulcrum The point a lever rests against in order to be able to move a load.

Geostationary orbit The path of an object moving at a high altitude around a planet so it does not move far from its position as seen from the surface.

In vitro fertilization Form of assisted (IVF) reproductive technology that brings sex cells, sperm, and ova together to be fertilized outside the body.

Kinetic To do with movement. For instance, kinetic energy is the energy stored in an object's movement, which is greater when it moves faster or when it is larger.

Mass The amount of stuff in an object, which is another way of saying the number of protons, neutrons, and electrons in an object. The more mass something has, the more it is pulled by gravity.

Molecule A group of atoms stuck together, which behave like one particle.

Nanotechnology Application of material science based on structures that are less than 100 nanometers in size.

Neolithic Revolution Also sometimes called the New Stone Age. Period around 10,000 years ago when human communities moved around less and developed new ways of growing food in smaller areas.

Plastic Materials made of strings of carbon-based molecules that can be molded and colored to suit a variety of applications.

Power How quickly energy can be transferred from one store to another.

Qubit Unit of information in quantum computers based on two states or positions of a particle, as well as the mathematics of an undecided mix of the states called a superposition.

Robot Programmable machine that can carry out specific tasks on its own in response to what it senses in its environment.

Smelting The process of heating metals mixed with other elements to separate out the metal.

Stem cells Basic cells that can develop characteristics that turn them into other cell types under the right conditions.

Technology Machines or activities that make tasks easier, often by automating a process, using scientific knowledge, doing it faster than a human is able to, or with a tool that can perform tasks that human bodies cannot do.

Transistor Device that boosts and switches currents by changing the conductivity of a connecting bridge of "semiconducting" material.

Work The force required to make an object displace by a certain distance.

X-ray High-frequency light waves that are commonly used to create images of dense material—such as bones—that can't be seen using the low-frequency light waves visible to the eye.

INDEX

CREDITS

Michael McRae: Engineering is such a vast, rich field of discovery and application. There are so many educators who have inspired my love of science and engineering and who deserve my gratitude, as my teacher, colleague, or inspiration. Special thanks to Dr. Graham Walker, for encouraging me to explore my creative side in developing hands-on activities; to Alom Shaha's inspiration when it comes to teaching engineering by using what one has at hand; and my wife, Liz, for helping me maintain my passion for communicating science and technology. A special thanks must also go to Ashleigh McRae, for her guiding hand in bioengineering ideas.

Jonathan Berliner: I would like to thank my lovely wife, Dr. Radha Kothari, for being patient with me while I wrote; Alom Shaha, for passing opportunities on; and to everyone who writes and checks Wikipedia articles, without whom I would know much, much less.

Images:
Unless otherwise noted, all images have been created by Tall Tree.

Shutterstock: 9, 30, 52, 70, 88, 108, 126, 146, 166, 178, 196, 212 Blan-k; 10–11 Jamila Aliyeva, AndriyA, Tribalium, Laurentiu Timplaru, Flat_Enot, piscary; 12–13 AndriyA, Tribalium, Laurentiu Timplaru, piscari; 16–17 Farid Huseynov, potatosapiens, andrerosi, VectorsMarket, VECTOR ICONS, Grimgram, howcolour; 18–19 Popcic, Macrovector, Sam Brannan, ONYXprj, gjebic Nicolae; 20–21 Macrovector; 24–25 Design tech art, angelh, BigMouse; 26–27 Lineicons freebird, unknown contributor, stas11, Gisele Yashar, UI, Sylfida, Martial Red, nexusby, aldebaran1; 28–29 Mr.Creative, Egor Shilov, FaithHopeLove, Premiumvectors, vectorlight, Michael Beetlov, Marnikus; 35–36 Farhad Bek, Titov Nikolai, Martial Red, travelfoto, vectorlight; 41 Nasky; 42 (T) GoTar, Designua; (C) Roupplar; (BL) jesadaphorn, (BR) Bohdana Seheda; 43 (TL) mehmetaligrafik; (TR), (B) Nikita_Petrov; 44–45 stockshoppe, sophielaliberte; 46 OSweetNature; 47 Varlamova Lydmila; 49 Amanita Silvicora; 50 unknown contributor, AVIcon, badrun13, Lukas Kurka, musmellow, Tzubasa, tatianasun, gritsalak karalak; 51 Fouad A. Saad, metamorworks, OsherR, BlueRingMedia; 56–57 cash1994; 59 gattopazzo; 60, 164 (L) Morphart Creation; 64, 65 A7880S; 69 VectorMine; 75 Inna Harlamoff; 76, 77 Shanvood; 78 Sergey Merkulov; 80–81 Jakinnboaz; 82 Studio BKK; 83, 143 gstraub; 84 Strejman; 85 Steve Cymro; 92 Colin Hayes; 94 attaphong; 95 fourth try; 96 (T) sharpner, VitalyVK; 99 Webspark; 101 Vectormine; 103–104 Naeblys; 105 peart; 106 Kit8.net; 107 (T) andrey_l, (B) Ico Maker; 113 Dzm1try, grmarc, Sentavio; 115 Fouad A. Saad; 117 VectorMine; 120 Dn Br; 123, 125 Designua; 130 N.Vinoth Narasingam; 134 Steve Cymro; 144 (L) Butusova Elena, (C) Tribalium, (R) Dario Sabljak; 145 (T) artsmith, (B) MarySan; 152, 153 Blamb; 154 Nikolayev Alexey; 157 Magicleaf; 159 TatyanaTVK; 161, Emre Terim; 163 Soleil Nordic; 164 (C) Rvector, (R) ShadeDesign; 165 (L) Ira Bagira; 177 Jemastock, elenabsl, Jemastock; 184 Lexanda; 185 Naeblys; 189 Emre Terim, metamorworks, My Portfolio; 191 Unitone Vector; 195 Fouad A. Saad; 200 (T–B) ART.ICON, Colorcocktail, WKung; 201 (T–B) crixtina, Titov Nikolai, Sergey Merkulov, VikiVector, Ivan Feoktistov; 202–203 jekson_js, Top Vector Studio, Dragana Eric, Morphart Creation, cash1994, Inna Harlamoff, Intellson; 204–205 DStarky, Jamila Aliyeva, ksenvitaln, Victor Z, Mario Breda, Ma Sua, Steinar; 206–207 kawano, Alongkorn Sanguansook, Cobisimo, Yaroslav Shkuro, RedKoala, kosmofish, Claudio Divizia, Marina Shevchenko, larionova Olga 11, In-Finity, Arizzona Design, freesoulproduction; 208–209 Olga Zakharova, Salim Nasirov, gjebic nicolae, struvictory, vectorlight, brgfx, MSSA, Rashad Ashur, Martial Red.

Other: 23 Sarah Skeate; 66-67 public domain; 86 public domain; 87 CC BY-SA 3.0 | Pjrensburg; 115 Michael Faraday| public domain; 119 Alamy| Photo12 Collection; 165 (R) CC BY-NC-SA 2.0 | Biodiversity Heritage Library; 187 Lindsey Johns; 206 (nuclear fission image) CC BY-SA 4.0 | MikeRun; 208 (oganesson image) CC BY-SA 4.0 | Maxskonborg; (airbus image) CC BY-SA 3.0 | Sabulyn; (smartphone image) CC BY 3.0 US | Milinda Courey, The Noun Project; (accelerator image) CC BY-SA 3.0 | BR84.